# FLAME IN MY HEART

David Adam is the Vicar of Holy Island where his work involves ministering to thousands of pilgrims and other visitors. He was born in Alnwick, Northumberland, and worked as a coal miner before being ordained. During more than twenty years as Vicar of Danby in North Yorkshire he discovered a gift for composing prayers in the Celtic pattern. Since 1985 he has published several very popular collections of prayers and meditations based on the Celtic tradition, using material he has tried and tested with groups and individuals from his own parishes and on retreat.

Also by David Adam:

*The Edge of Glory: Prayers in the Celtic tradition*
(Triangle 1985)

*The Cry of the Deer: Meditations on the hymn of St Patrick*
(Triangle 1987)

*Tides and Seasons: Modern prayers in the Celtic tradition*
(Triangle 1989)

*The Eye of the Eagle: Meditations on the hymn 'Be thou my vision'*
(Triangle 1990)

*Border Lands: The Best of David Adam*
(SPCK 1991)

*Power Lines: Celtic prayers about work*
(Triangle 1992)

*Fire of the North: The Illustrated Life of St Cuthbert*
(SPCK 1993)

*The Open Gate: Celtic prayers for growing spiritually*
(Triangle 1994)

*The Rhythm of Life: Celtic Daily Prayer*
(Triangle 1996)

# FLAME IN
# MY HEART

St Aidan for Today

————

DAVID ADAM

————

*Illustrations by*
*Jean Freer*

**TRIANGLE**

First published 1997
Triangle
SPCK
Holy Trinity Church
Marylebone Road
London NW1 4DU

*British Library Cataloguing in Publication Data*
A catalogue record for this book is available
from the British Library

ISBN 0-281-05033-3

Typeset by Pioneer Associates, Perthshire
Printed and bound in Great Britain by
Caledonian International Book Manufacturing Ltd.
Glasgow

# Contents

# Introduction

When I was a boy, whenever we travelled north on the A1 road or by rail into Scotland, my father would point out a fairy-tale-like castle rising out of the sea and say, 'That's the Holy Island of Lindisfarne.' This became a ritual as we passed by; sometimes he would say, 'That's the island of the saints.' I would look at the long strip of land stretching out in the sea and wondered if it belonged to the same world as I did; sometimes it seemed very near and at other times far away. I hoped to go there one day. I never dreamed that one day I would live there.

As I grew older, my father would tell me stories about Aidan and Cuthbert, heroes in life and in prayer. Years later, he took me across the sands, before the causeway was built, to see the Island and feel its history. I was aware of great stretches of sand, of bright sunlight and countless sea birds. I watched pole after pole as we passed by the 'Pilgrim's Way'. The castle rising from its rock was straight out of a medieval romance and still stirs the hearts of many by its idyllic setting. The carved stones in the old museum were strange and fascinating, I liked tracing the Celtic knotwork patterns with my fingers. But what stayed with me forever was the story of the saints. They were so different, so full of wonder, I felt they must have been giants of men.

Later still I would become even more impressed by their lifestyle, their holiness, their concern for the poor and their efforts at reconciliation between peoples. 'Here', said a friend and lover of these island saints, 'is the Saint Francis before Saint Francis.' I knew what he meant. Before the great saint of Assisi taught us a love for the world, saints like Aidan showed us a love for all about him. Aidan wrestling with demons but at one with much of nature. Aidan who gave his horse away to a beggar. Aidan who refused to ride because it placed him above others. He walked the lanes and taught people to meditate. Aidan who bought slaves to give them their freedom, and then housed and educated them if they so required. Lindisfarne had a school where royalty and slaves were educated together. Then there was Cuthbert, who had otters dry his feet after he prayed all night in cross-vigil. Cuthbert who shared with the rooks and cared for the eider ducks. Cuthbert who was fed by an eagle. Story after story has been told of these holy men of God who were at one with their surroundings and who communicated to the people about them. These were men who helped to build up kingdoms and to weave in the kingdom of heaven. They dedicated the Island as a place of God's presence and peace. Little did I dream that this Holy Island would become my home, that I would worship where the saints have worshipped, that I would meet the countless pilgrims who come to this holy place. I had hoped to live near the sea, but I did not ask God to drop me into it!

Lindisfarne is a small island but its influence on the history of England and Europe is all out of proportion to its size. Here were a great school and monastery that would influence the minds of the English for generations. From here men went out to convert the English and parts of the continent of Europe. Names trip off the tongue; Aidan, Cuthbert, Chad, Cedd and Wilfrid, to mention only a few.

They were to go out and convert the pagan English. Cuthbert was at Melrose and Ripon, and as bishop across at Carlisle. Cedd became the bishop of the East Saxons and his little church at Bradwell-on-Sea still stands. He also built the monastery at Lastingham in North Yorkshire. Chad was the first bishop of Lichfield. Wilfrid built the great church at Hexham, was bishop of York. He founded monasteries in the Leicester area. He also spent much time preaching on the continent. It is said that he taught the West Saxons to fish with nets.

These men were apostolic pioneers, builders of monasteries, schools and churches, men of great courage and dedication who shaped the course of England. Yet they were men with their feet firmly on the ground. When the Vikings attacked the Island in 793 Alcuin wrote, 'Behold the church of Saint Cuthbert spattered with the blood of the priests of God, despoiled of all its ornaments. A place more venerable than all in Britain is given prey to pagan peoples.' So often it has been looked upon as a very special holy place, 'more venerable than all in Britain'. Even recently in a television broadcast Rabbi Lionel Blue said, 'Of all of holy England, Holy Island is the holiest of all.' There certainly seem to be more saints per square inch on the Island than you can find almost anywhere else. Even today something of this has remained, there is a sanctity that has lingered. People still come because it is a holy place, a special place in their own personal history. People come and are inspired, some are never the same again. It is still a place to stretch oneself and to extend one's vision.

Lindisfarne is only one-and-a-quarter miles from the shore as the crow flies. As it is a tidal island it can only be approached with safety when the tide is out. This gives a rhythm to life: in the summer it means times of extreme business when thousands come, but the tide will close in and the majority will go. In August a thousand people a day, and more, visit the parish church. There is a growing interest in the Celtic saints and in the Golden Age of Northumbria. Day by day I meet people interested in the Island saints, people who want to know more – and to tell me what they know. Many are discovering a lost heritage, a treasure which is their own but which has been long forgotten. Here is an authentic lifestyle, a purpose for living, a way of love and dedication that can guide us as well as the poles guide pilgrims across the sands. In all of this seeking and searching for pointers to authentic living, Aidan's example looms large.

Aidan certainly deserves to be better known among the saints of this land. He is one of the great founding fathers of the church. In his book *Leaders of the Northern Church*, Bishop Lightfoot of Durham wrote, 'Augustine is the apostle of Kent, but Aidan is the apostle of England.' This was taken up by Alfred Fryer in his book with the title *Aidan, Apostle of England*. He wrote, 'May we not claim for Aidan the first place in the evangelization of our race?' With the revived interest in the Celtic saints, Aidan is at last coming to the fore.

There is no doubt that the Celtic period in the church was one of great enthusiasm and amazing outreach, an outreach not only to make new Christians but to regain the lapsed. From this period there are many lessons we can learn for today. Bede in his *History of the English Church and People* said of Aidan, 'His life is in marked contrast with the apathy of our own times.' I believe those words are as true now as when they were written.

Aidan has much to teach us. His attitude to possessions could lead many to freedom. His making God his priority, and his concern for foundations, has much to say to our frenetic times. We can learn so much from his gentleness and openness. His seeing the Christ in others is life-transforming. The insights that say, 'If you are to change a nation you must change the attitude of its leaders', or 'To win ordinary people you cannot tower above them', show a greater understanding and humility than many modern plans and projects. I have no hesitation in commending this great man of God to you as a guide and a soul friend.

This book has been born out of talking with thousands of people, listening to lectures and giving them. Parts arose out of taking retreats and other parts out of talking to the countless children who come to Lindisfarne for an experience of the saints. Some of it obviously arises from my deep Celtic heritage and the folk stories I learned as a child. All of it is influenced by my deep love for this little Island and its inhabitants of today as well as the past. I am truly blessed to be part of so rich a heritage, and want it to enrich the present.

The first two chapters are before Aidan arrives. In these I have allowed my own experiences and feeling for Northumbria to take a good deal of the space. In this way I hope that I have set the scene for what is to follow. From chapter 3, I have tried to let Aidan speak for himself through his lifestyle and example. The source for all the chapters is mainly Bede's *History of the English Church and People*; this provides the skeleton. I have had to flesh this out through Celtic material that was relevant to the times of Aidan; without this there could be no story. I have also looked at some of the early

Anglo-Saxon poetry, as Aidan must have heard at least some of this. When you discover that the only prayer of Aidan's we have on record is, 'Lord, see what evil Penda does', you realize a lot of fleshing out had to be done! However, I have sought to stick closely to the thought patterns of the Celts and of the times.

At the end of each chapter there is a quotation from Bede's *History of the English Church and People*; this looks at what has gone before. After that there is a psalm, or portion of a psalm, which is there to recite and to learn. Learning off by heart is an important part of the 'Exercises'. Then follows a meditation which it is hoped will be extended by the reader. To get into a daily pattern of meditation is important if we are to grow in the faith. Finally there is a prayer to focus all before the Divine Presence. We must get ourselves talking to God rather than about Him. I have tried in these Exercises to follow what Bede says of Aidan: 'All who accompanied him, whether monks or layfolk, were required to meditate, that is, either to read the Scriptures or learn the Psalms.'

There is no doubt that the love of God burned in the heart of Aidan and shone out beyond the Dark Ages. His faith and example can be a great light to our times, until we burn with the same fire and are engulfed in the love of God.

## Family Tree of the Kings of Bernicia and Deira

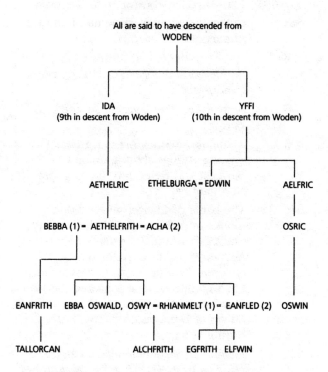

All are said to have descended from
WODEN

IDA
(9th in descent from Woden)

YFFI
(10th in descent from Woden)

AETHELRIC    ETHELBURGA = EDWIN    AELFRIC

BEBBA (1) = AETHELFRITH = ACHA (2)    OSRIC

EANFRITH    EBBA    OSWALD, OSWY = RHIANMELT (1) = EANFLED (2)    OSWIN

TALLORCAN    ALCHFRITH    EGFRITH    ELFWIN

In the interest of simplicity, I have only included the names that are mentioned in this book and have a bearing on the time of Aidan. The names of the kingdoms of Bernicia and Deira are of Celtic origin. Deira stretched from the Humber to the Tees. For most of the time of Aidan the kingdom of Bernicia area would be from the Tees to the Firth of Forth.

# Time Chart

| | |
|---|---|
| 547–593 | Ida, 'The Flamebearer', rules Bernicia. |
| 565 | Columba arrives from Ireland to found the monastery of Iona. |
| c.590 | Urien ap Rheged, a Christian king, murdered at the siege of Inis Metcaud (Lindisfarne). |
| 593 | Aethelfrith, 'The Twister', succeeds to Bernicia. |
| 603 | Aethelfrith marries Acha of Deira. This marriage brings about a union of Bernicia and Deira into the kingdom of Northumbria. |
| 616 | The battle of Chester where 1,000 monks from Bangor are killed at prayer. The battle of the river Idle where Aethelfrith is killed. Aethelfrith's children, Eanfrith, Oswald, Oswy and Ebba go into exile at Iona and the kingdom of Dalriada.<br>Edwin of Deira succeeds to all of Northumbria. |
| 625 | Edwin marries Ethelburga, a Christian princess from Kent. She brings with her Paulinus as her chaplain.<br>Baptism of Edwin's daughter Eanfled. |
| 627 | Baptism of Edwin and Hild at York. Conversion of Northumbria by Paulinus. |
| 632 | Death of Edwin at Hatfield Chase. Paulinus and Queen Ethelburga flee the kingdom. |

|       | Eanfrith and Osric seek to take over Bernicia and Deira. |
|-------|------------------------------------------------------------|
| 633   | Eanfrith and Osric are killed. |
| 634   | Oswald defeats Penda and kills Cadwallon at the battle of Heavenfield on Hadrian's Wall near Hexham. Oswald invites a mission from Iona to Northumbria. Corman arrives but soon returns to Iona. |
| 635   | Aidan arrives at Bamburgh and begins the monastery on Lindisfarne. |
| 642   | Oswald killed by Penda at Oswestry. Oswy succeeds to Bernicia and Oswin to Deira. Both continue to support the Lindisfarne mission. |
| 643   | Oswy marries Eanfled in an attempt to unite the two kingdoms. |
| c.650 | Penda attacks Bamburgh. |
| 651   | Oswin is assassinated at the instigation of Oswy, the kingdoms still do not unite. Aidan dies at Bamburgh and is buried on Lindisfarne. Finan becomes the Bishop of Lindisfarne. Cuthbert has a vision at the death of Aidan and enters the monastery at Melrose. |
| 652   | Death of Segene, abbot of Iona and friend of Oswald. |

# List of Principal Characters

## AT IONA

*Columba*  The first abbot of Iona and missionary to the Picts 563–579.

*Segene*  The fifth abbot of Iona and friend of Oswald 623–652.

*Corman*  The first missionary from Iona to Northumbria at the request of Oswald. This mission failed in 634/5.

*Aidan*  Second missionary from Iona to Northumbria. Sets up at Lindisfarne in 635.

## AT LINDISFARNE

*Aidan*  First bishop and abbot of Lindisfarne 635–651.

*Cedd,*
*Cynebil,*
*Caelin,*
*Chad*  Four Anglican brothers all trained at Lindisfarne. All became priests. Cedd and Chad became bishops. Cedd worked with the Mercians at the invitation of Peada son of Penda and then with the East Saxons. Cedd founded Lastingham monastery in North Yorkshire. He acted as the interpreter at the Synod of Whitby in 664. Chad succeeded his brother as abbot of Lastingham. For a short while he was bishop of York. He established a monastery at

xvi

|            | Barrow (Lincs) and another close to Lichfield Cathedral where he was bishop for three years. |
| :--------- | :----------------------------------------------------------------------------------------------- |
| *Cudda*    | Was from the court of Oswald, living on Lindisfarne, being looked after by Wilfrid. |
| *Wilfrid*  | Was educated at Lindisfarne. Encouraged by Queen Eanfled he went to Canterbury and then Rome where he studied under Archdeacon Boniface. Was the leader of the Roman party at the Synod of Whitby in 664. |

## IN NORTHUMBRIA

|               | |
| :------------ | :--- |
| *Aethelfrith* | Grandson of Ida, king of Bernicia, and followed him in the kingship in 593. He married Acha of Deira in 603 and united the two kingdoms into Northumbria. His children were Eanfrith, Oswald, Oswy and Ebba. |
| *Edwin*       | A prince of the dynasty of Deira, had been driven into exile by Aethelfrith. On victory over Aethelfrith, with help from Raedwald of the East Angles, Edwin entered the whole kingdom of Northumbria, driving into exile Eanfrith, Oswald, Oswy and Ebba. Edwin married Ethelburga, a Christian princess from Kent. She brought with her Paulinus as her chaplain. |

| | |
|---|---|
| *Eanfled* | The daughter of Edwin and Ethelburga, was baptized by Paulinus in 626. In 642 Eanfled married Oswy of Bernicia; it was hoped this would reunite the two kingdoms. She was Wilfrid's patron. |
| *Hild* | When Edwin was baptized by Paulinus in York, so was Hild. For thirty-three years she lived a secular life. She then decided to go to France to become a nun. Aidan persuaded Hild to stay and she founded a monastery on the north bank of the river Wear. She then went to Hartlepool and later to Whitby. |
| *Eanfrith* | Son of Aethelfrith and Bebba. Driven into exile by Edwin. Killed by Cadwallon in 633. |
| *Oswald* | Son of Aethelfrith and Acha, defeated Penda and Cadwallon at Heavenfield 634. Invited the Iona mission to Northumbria. Acted as interpreter for Aidan. Killed by Penda at Oswestry 642. Relics were at Bamburgh and Lindisfarne. |
| *Oswy* | Son of Aethelfrith and Acha, succeeded Oswald to Bernicia. Friend of Aidan and the Lindisfarne mission. Married Eanfled to unite the two kingdoms. Assassinated Oswin of Deira to unite the kingdoms but this unification did not happen. |

| | |
|---|---|
| *Rhianmelt* | First wife of Oswy and a princess from Rheged; her name means 'Queen of Lightning'. |
| *Ebba* | Sister of Eanfrith, Oswald and Oswy, later to found the monastery at St Abb's head. |
| *Tallorcan* | Son of Eanfrith and a Pictish princess. He became a king of the Picts. |
| *Oswin* | Friend of Aidan of Lindisfarne. Man of culture. King of Deira. He gave Aidan a horse as a special gift. He was assassinated by the reeve Aethelwin at the instigation of Oswy. |

OTHER

| | |
|---|---|
| *Penda* | A pagan king, a ferocious warlord and slayer of at least five kings including Eanfrith and Oswald. Penda's tribe were the Mierce, that is the 'Borderfolk' of the border between England and Wales and laid the foundations of Mercia. He attacked Bamburgh in 650. |
| *Cadwallon* | King of Gwynedd, no doubt a Christian. He was trying to stop the expansionist policies of the Anglo-Saxons. He was killed at the battle of Heavenfield in 634. |

## *Life is a Battle*

Life is a battle. There are conflicts around us and within us all our lives. Yet if we are at war we are at least alive. If the warfare has ceased, we must ask if we too have ceased really to live. There are times when we are really up against it and we wonder if we will survive; tensions, set-backs, opposition, weariness, weakness all seem regularly to come to diminish us. I was struggling to survive, or so it felt. I had tried to escape, but all the things I had run away from had followed me. In truth, some of them I was carrying inside me. There was no getting away from them. The powers that were against me seemed stronger than those that were for me. Wave upon wave seemed to rush at me, I thought that I would soon be overwhelmed. Prayer would not come. I was work-weary and tempest-tossed. My well-being was once more threatened by forces larger than I. In my desperation the only words that would come to mind were those of the Breton fisherman: 'Lord, the sea is so large and my boat is so small.'

All this was happening in idyllic surroundings, in fact the area was called Heavenfield. It was in the good walking country along Hadrian's Roman Wall. There was the little church of St Oswald-in-Lee and a splendid row of sycamore trees. From here you could look over a magnificently wide panorama of Northumberland. It was a place for extending one's vision. There was more to see than the eye could take in. The expanse of the sky was breathtaking. Unusually, even the blue line of the Cheviot hills in the distance failed to cheer me. I turned and walked towards the road and a large stone cross. Someone had placed a beautiful collection of early summer flowers at its foot. This was a place of battles, for the cross commemorated the battle of Oswald to

2

gain his kingdom in AD 634. It was a battle not only for land but to gain the hearts and minds of men: a battle for two kingdoms, one earthly and the other of heaven.

Oswald is one of the great heroes of the north, straight out of the pages of romance. His story might have been told in an epic poem in the fashion of *Beowulf*, a tale of heroic wrestling against dragons and darkness. As a child Oswald grew up in a palace. His father, the mighty warrior Aethelfrith, had captured the kingdom of Deira and united it with his own Bernicia, so laying the foundation for the kingdom of Northumbria. In the process many of the native British had been driven out of their lands or killed. Aethelfrith transformed what had begun as a small pirate band based at Bamburgh into the mightiest military power in northern Britain.

This was a time of small kingdoms and regular warfare, mostly small tribal battles. Aethelfrith was killed by Raedwald, perhaps by the very sword that is in the Sutton Hoo collection in the British Museum. In 616 Edwin took over Northumbria, driving the four children of Aethelfrith into exile. Eanfrith, Oswald, Oswy and Ebba were all taken northwards for safety. The oldest, Eanfrith, later married a Pictish princess and his son Tallorcan became king of the Picts. It would seem that Oswald and Oswy, with their sister Ebba, went to the west of Scotland, to the Irish Celtic kingdom of Dalriada in Argyll. There seems no doubt that the twelve-year-old Oswald with Ebba and Oswy were at this time given a sound Christian education. The boys spent some time on the island of Iona with the Columban monks; Ebba was more likely educated on the nearby 'Island of Women', Eilean non

Ban. As Oswald grew it would be essential that he learned the art of warfare; he probably spent as much time, if not more, at the stronghold of Dunadd as at Iona. Eanfrith, Oswald and Oswy would all have to be prepared for the day they might come into their kingdom. Their exile was to last for seventeen years, during which the young men grew up, and were trained to be leaders of people.

Edwin was killed at the battle of Hatfield Chase by the alliance of Penda of Mercia and Cadwallon of Gwynedd, in the year 632. It was soon time for the children of Aethelfrith to return. Eanfrith came south with twelve thanes and a British-Celtic warband, probably hoping to make an alliance with the Christian British leader Cadwallon. But though he came to sue for peace, instead he and his men were put to the sword. Cadwallon was not in the mood for dealing with the children of Aethelfrith. The early hopes for the kingdom of Northumbria were being shattered. Now it was Oswald's turn to come south. He marched against Penda and Cadwallon with an army much smaller than that of his enemies; many of the trained leaders of Northumbria had already been killed along with Eanfrith. Oswald's chance of survival was in great doubt; common sense would have told him to return to the north.

The battlefield was to be on the land where I was now standing, the beautiful Heavenfield. Here Oswald and his men pitched their camp and waited, restoring their energies whilst Cadwallon and Penda came northwards. It was December and the cold night air would be testing enough for both sides. There were wild beasts in the forest below, the direction from which the enemy would come. The

4

mist rose in the valley. During the waiting, as he slept, Oswald had a vision of St Columba. The founder of Iona announced that Oswald would be king. He then reminded him of some words of God to Joshua at the river Jordan: 'Be strong and of good courage. Behold I shall be with you. Be determined and confident, for you will be the leader of these people as they occupy this land.' Then the saint added, 'March out this following night from your camp to battle, for on this occasion the Lord has granted to me that your foes shall be put to flight.' Perhaps it was a dawn attack that helped to give the army of Oswald the upper hand. The little army would have used the advantage of the higher ground to take their enemies by surprise. Oswald knew that, like Joshua, he must be strong in the Lord. Victory would be due to God alone. Before the battle he would set up the sign of the holy cross. Like the great emperor Constantine, who won his battle after seeing the sign of the cross, Oswald prayed to God, that in this sign he might conquer the enemy. A cross was quickly put together from two young trees rough hewn, and a hole was made ready for it to stand in. Oswald, fired by his vision and faith, seized the cross and placed it in the hole, holding it upright with both hands, until the soldiers heaped up the soil and made it fast in the ground. Fired with ecstasy, he then raised his voice and said to the whole army, 'Let us all kneel together and pray to the Almighty, the everliving and true God, to defend us in his mercy from a proud and cruel enemy. He knows that the war we have engaged in for the deliverance of our people is a just war.' They then advanced against the enemy silently in the swirling mists of the morning. Many of their foes had hardly time to take up their swords. Others fled in panic. The opposition was defeated and Cadwallon was killed.

All felt that this was a sign. The little army had defeated the larger one, just like Joshua's triumph at Jericho. Oswald had no doubt promised before the battle that if he and his men survived, his kingdom would become Christian. This would be how he would gain support from the men of Dalriada. In thanksgiving for the victory and as a means of uniting the British and the Anglo-Saxons, he sent to Iona for teachers of the Christian faith. He sought their learning for his court, as well as their Christian teaching.

As a Northumbrian, I knew this heroic story off by heart. But today it affected me in a new way. I heard again the wise words from Joshua: 'Be strong and of good courage. Behold I shall be with you.' Like Oswald, I let the words vibrate in my being. They in turn led me to St Paul and his exhortation to 'Be strong in the Lord and in the power of His might'. I knew I was not alone struggling against great forces, I had the power and the presence of God available to me. In my foolishness I had ignored the presence of the Almighty. I had tried to stand alone, and so felt as if I were alone. Like some weary giant, I was trying to carry the world on my shoulders. I had to remind myself once again that our feelings are often liars, moods and emotions can lead us astray. I was not on my own, I had great resources and, thank God, those resources were not dependent on me. Now some words of St Julian of Norwich came to mind to encourage me: 'He did not say, "You shall not be tempest-tossed, you shall not be work-weary, you shall not be discomforted." But He did say, "You shall not be overcome."'

I stood looking at the cross erected in memory of the battle of Heavenfield and the great Lenten hymn to the cross came to mind, with the words, 'The cross does chase all evil; before it darkness flieth.' Again I sought to trust in the power of God to defend and save. I placed between myself and my troubles the power of the cross of Christ.

> I put between me and all evil
> The saving power of God.
> I put between me and all darkness
> The saving power of God.
> I put between me and all weakness
> The saving power of God.
> I put between me and all terror
> The saving power of God.
> I put between me and destruction
> The saving power of God.
> I put between me and death
> The saving power of God.

What was I doing? I asked myself. Was this some sort of magic to make God act? Was I trying to monopolize or manipulate God? No. In meditating on the cross, and in prayer, I was acting out of realities of which I had lost sight. The truth is that God loves me, that God is with me, that God wants to help me. I had become blind and insensitive to this reality. I needed to awaken my senses, to teach my emotions. I needed to open myself to God. Above all, I needed to know that nothing could separate me from the love of God in Christ Jesus. Though my faith was weak it was faith in an almighty God, a saving God, who promised that I 'should not perish but have everlasting life'. I had to trust in Him more, I had to assure myself that He cares, that He is with me and is concerned about my well-being. This I did in front of the cross at Heavenfield.

To the north the clouds were gathering, black and threatening, yet where I stood it was warm and the sun was still shining. I knew the brightness would not last, but at that moment I felt I had learned a little more of the love and the grace of God and how He gives us strength to stand against the forces of evil. This was not an escape from the battle. I was only too well aware of the words, 'In the world you will have tribulation.' But I was also aware that the Christ went on to say, 'But be of good cheer, I have overcome the world.' I was not alone in the battle, and even if I lost a few rounds I knew that through Him victory was assured. This must be allowed to influence the way I live. At the same time I had to be aware that in this good world much of what should belong to God is under enemy occupation.

We must never belittle the powers of evil and destruction; if we do, they will overwhelm us. C. S. Lewis had this warning for us who live in an age when we often either pretend evil does not exist or get obsessed by it: 'There are two equal and opposite errors into which our race can fall about the devils. One is to disbelieve in their existence. The other is to believe, and to feel an excessive and unhealthy interest in them. They themselves are equally pleased by both errors and hail a materialist or a magician with the same delight.'[1] We do need to be aware that forces exist which could destroy us, and to commit ourselves to the power and love of God. We need to know that we are not personally almighty – in fact we know well that we are weak and fragile. But our God is almighty, all-powerful, and he cares for us.

8

So long as we are alive we are bound to be caught up in battles; the very effort of extending ourselves must often be a struggle. Once we cease to extend ourselves, to reach out, we stagnate and are on the road to death. A friend of mine when asked, 'How are you?' always replied, 'Battling on.' He was an old soldier and he once said to me, 'Never complain about the battle, if you are battling you are still alive. There are too many for whom the struggle is over.' Let us learn to rejoice when we are caught up in the active elements of the world, when everything is stirring around us. It is good to be where things are happening.

Another friend, from a friary, once confessed to me something he was finding very difficult. 'I find women attractive,' he said. I had to pause for a while before I could answer this one, it had such far-reaching consequences. Eventually I said, 'Thank God, brother. The day you stop finding women attractive, you will be dead, or something in you will have died.' There was a wonderful release of laughter from both of us at such a statement. But, I believe here was something of great importance. To kill those feelings was to destroy something that was truly human. To find the opposite sex attractive is part of rejoicing in life and is good. There is nothing wicked in this attraction, in fact it is very healthy. Certainly there are times when it can become obsessive or perverted, but that is when we have let it go wrong. As a monk, my friend would often have to wrestle with this – but at least he was alive. Even temptations are about our potential, about what we are able to do. If we feel tempted towards something we cannot do, it is more likely to be fantasy than temptation.

In this case we rejoiced that this young friar was

alive and found life so full of goodness! But that was not to deny that life can be a constant battle. It is easy to lower standards and compromise ourselves. It is necessary to choose a path if we are not to end up lost. It is no use wandering from one direction to another; we need to decide who we are and where we want to go. Then we have to dedicate ourselves to it. God's words to Joshua that Oswald heard should be looked at in their context. 'Be strong and courageous', be careful to observe God's commandments, remember them, speak of them, obey them; do not be fearful, do not be discouraged; 'and the Lord will be with you wherever you go'. It is not surprising that the Celtic Christians often called themselves 'soldiers of Christ'. They acknowledged that they were in a battle for the coming in of a Kingdom. They knew that they were under orders, that they had to accept discipline. They also declared that 'in that warfare there was no end'.

Oswald was willing to die for a cause. It is better to die *for* something than *of* something. Life needs a purpose. One of the saddest comments on our times is that there are so many people without any purpose or goal. Such people are adrift with no destination. They are tossed to and fro by whatever wind that blows. Life is often wasted away in idle fantasy. We need aims and objectives if we are to get anywhere. Because we live in the age of the anti-hero, it is very difficult to extend ourselves or dedicate ourselves. The world will forever say, 'Why bother?' We need to know that if we do not aim high, we will not reach high. Without commitment on our part nothing will happen. Without discipline there will be no discipling.

Oswald was not afraid to commit himself to the

cause he felt he was called to. He knew that it could involve total commitment and even death. He was willing to give of himself and of his goods, and in so doing he enriched many who were around him. Time and time again he would show his generosity, his openness of hand, and his ability to be with his people. He believed that you can only avoid warfare by being prepared for it. If you have a strong front you can often help people to live in peace. Oswald in his goodness helped to begin the 'Golden Age' for Northumbria. Amidst what came to be called the Dark Ages, Oswald's kingdom was to become a centre of learning and Christian outreach.

## EXERCISES

'When King Oswald was about to give battle to the heathen, he set up the sign of the holy cross, and kneeling down, asked God that He would grant His heavenly aid.' Bede 3.2

1. If your life is a tough battle, think on these words from Psalm 91.1–4, and learn them:

He who dwells in the shelter of the Most High:
    who abides under the shadow of the
    Almighty,
he will say to the Lord:
'You are my refuge, and my stronghold:
    my God in whom I trust.'
For He will deliver you from the snare of the
hunter:

and from the destroying curse.
He will cover you with His wings,
and you will be safe under His feathers:
>His faithfulness will be your shield and
>defence . . .

2. 'The message about Christ's death on the cross
is nonsense to those who are being lost: but for
us who are being saved it is God's power.'
1 Corinthians 1.18

Slowly and thoughtfully make the sign of the
cross, upon yourself. Say the words from the bap-
tismal service.

>I sign you with the cross, the sign of Christ.
>Do not be ashamed to confess the faith of
>    Christ crucified.
>Fight valiantly under the banner of Christ
>    against sin, the world, and the devil,
>and continue his faithful soldier and servant to
>    the end of your life.[2]

Use this as a means of tuning in to, becoming aware
of, the great love of God towards you.

Let the cross be a sign of your deliverance, your
freedom.

You may like to add, 'Jesus Christ is the light of
the world, a light that no darkness can quench.'

Allow the saving power of God to be at work in
your life.

Let His power come to your weakness.

Let His love come to your loneliness.

Let His hope dispel your fears.

Let His peace bring calm to your troubles.

May you find in the cross of Christ Jesus

A sure ground for your faith.

A firm support for your hopes,

An assurance that light conquers darkness,
And that love is stronger than death.

3. Ask yourself, are you really learning to be 'strong in the Lord', or are you still reliant on your own powers alone? Learn to put more trust in God. Take to heart the words from Joshua: 'Remember that I have commanded you to be determined and confident! Don't be afraid or discouraged, for I, the Lord your God, am with you wherever you go.' Joshua 1.9

4. Pray this prayer of Jeremy Taylor:

Grant, O Lord, that in Thy wounds, I may find
    my safety,
in Thy stripes my cure,
in Thy pain my peace,
in Thy cross my victory,
in Thy resurrection my triumph,
and a crown of righteousness in the glories of
    Thy eternal kingdom.

*The Open Door*

Living on a tidal island has taught me a lot of things. Having to adjust to daily tides sharpens your mind. You can only leave the island of Lindisfarne when the causeway is open; if you hang about making your mind up whether to go or not, you can miss your chance. If you hover about and wonder 'if', the tide turns on you and the opportunity is gone – perhaps for ever. In all our lives there are things we must do when the opportunity arises, or we will not get another chance. The often quoted lines from Shakespeare's *Julius Caesar* come to mind:

> There is a tide in the affairs of men,
> Which, taken at the flood, leads on to fortune;
> Omitted, all the voyage of their life
> Is bound in shallows and in miseries.[1]

Corman of Iona is remembered as the man who missed his chance, a man who was not aware when the tide turned. No one will ever know what caused Corman to give up on his mission, but we remember he did not fulfil it. A door of opportunity had been opened in Northumbria, and Corman decided to close it. A nation was being opened up to the gospel, and Corman decided to retreat. It was an opportunity to win a kingdom for Christ and he chose to return to Iona.

Oswald's exile had been a good training ground in the Christian faith. An earthly kingdom had closed to him, yet the greater kingdom of heaven opened up to him. His exile on Iona began as a loss, but it would prove an inestimable gain. When he became king, he promised, his people would have not only teaching in the faith, but a wider education, books, freedom, and the great uniting power that Christianity could bring. He wanted them

16

to experience the riches of the kingdom of God. He was forever saying that if he came to his kingdom, it would become Christian. Oswald of Northumbria was true to his promise. He asked his dear friend Segene, abbot of Iona, to send him teachers. The military support he had received from the kingdom of Dalriada had probably had the proviso that, if they were victorious, the kingdom would become Christian.

Out of all the monks of Iona, Corman was chosen for this special mission, to bring the Angles of Northumbria to Christ. No one believed that this would be an easy task. No doubt Corman was chosen because he was a powerful leader and strong in the faith. Corman led a trusty band of teaching monks. After a journey of ten days or more, they arrived at Bamburgh. The fortress, set upon a great rock, was a symbol of Oswald's power. It was a typical Anglican settlement, full of war heroes and men of valour. There would be tales of raids and adventures. There would be a good deal of drinking and sharing out of booty after raids. None of this would be totally new to a Celtic monk. A greater difficulty was that these men had recently been slayers of Christians. In 603, Oswald's father Aethelfrith had attacked and defeated Aedan mac Gabhrain of the Dalriada at Degastan. Even Cadwallon's death at Heavenfield must have been a matter of regret to many of the Celtic monks. There were deep and good relationships between the Irish Celtic Christians and the British Celtic Christians. True, Oswald and some of the leaders had accepted Christianity but his was obviously a heathen kingdom, and to the British the Angles were the enemy of occupation.

Yet Corman accepted his task as a great honour.

He had the chance to win a kingdom for Christ. If these warriors accepted the faith, it could be a great uniting power in the land. A great door was opened to Corman, but he felt that the people were barbarian. He was no doubt wearied with his journey. He found the language of the Angles difficult. Inside the palace there was a certain hostility from some of the young warriors. These Angles were the murderers of monks and the plunderers of local people. Their ideals were linked with killing and battles. Even their heaven was a place of warriors and war. They were not the stuff that Christians were made of. Corman was given the chance to transform a kingdom, but he was a hard man. The demands he made were too much. Neither side seemed to understand the other, and there was little willingness to bend on either side. Corman was determined to subdue the Angles and make them obey. But this was not acceptable to these warriors. They wanted their lives extended, not diminished, and who was this man who sought to command them? Neither one nor the other was able to give way or find some common ground.

It was not long before Corman and his companions were back on Iona. It must have come as a shock to Abbot Segene and many of the monks to see Corman return. How would Oswald react now that his offer had been rebuffed? A great door had been generously opened and Corman had slammed it shut. He just could not tolerate the barbaric ways of the Angles, they were too brutish to learn anything. He brought home tales of them killing the old, the weak and the handicapped. It was no use preaching to them, they were too uncivilized and stubborn. Corman recalled that Oswald's father had been called 'the Twister' by the British because of his double dealings. He also reminded the brothers that the Twister had caused the death of a thousand monks at Chester, just because they were praying. The very founder of the kingdom of Bernicia Ida, had boasted the name 'Flamebearer' because of the number of villages he had fired. As Corman went on, it was clear that he was very angry about his own need to return. Obviously ashamed at having to come back, he railed against those who had invited him as if they were beasts. He had developed a hostility towards the very people who were seeking to offer him hospitality.

Here was a warrior king who had asked to be taught more of the faith. Oswald was already a Christian and was willing to deepen his commitment and understanding. Many of those in the palace were already willing to commit themselves, even if initially it was simply to please their king. When we consider Oswald's generosity, his prayer life, and his own willingness to act as translator, it must have seemed that the door had swung wide open. But something stopped Corman making any progress. It makes us wonder what Corman was looking for. Obviously there would be no instant results. Yet the climate seemed favourable. True, the palace was nothing like the monastic settlement on Iona, but surely that was why he had been invited.

Too often, mission has wanted to change people into the image of the missionary. Too often, whole races and peoples have lost the richness of their culture in the name of Christian mission. The later blossoming of the Hiberno-English culture in the Golden Age of Northumbria was proof of what was waiting to be discovered. Too often, in the name of Christ we have forced people to accept what we want rather than listen to them. If we are truly to lead a person to Christ we must accept them where they are, and walk for a while in their shoes. The very image of our God is that He came down where we are, into our situation. The Christ came to serve rather than be served, and to give His life as a ransom for many. It was while we were yet sinners that He died for us.

We must accept people as they are. They are not trophies to be gained or numbers to be added to our lists. Each person has an individual experience and that can enrich ours as much as we can enrich theirs. It is too easy to deplore what we do not like, or to demand that they conform to the image that we want. This is far from 'the glorious liberty of the children of God'. The very diversity of peoples and nations is what enriches and adds colour to our world.

There is something even more important at stake. We must ask ourselves if we are going as possessors, as if we had a monopoly of Christ, as if He was with us and with no other. So much of our mission has been as 'owners of God' to those who are dispossessed. We have seen ourselves as the rich going to the poor, as the wise going to the ignorant.

Let me give you an illustration. When I was a young curate, I was asked to go and visit an old lady who was dying. I was fresh out of theological college and full of heroics – actually it was arrogance! I saw her need, and decided to take Christ to her. But, when I got there I discovered something I was to discover again and again: I could not take Christ because he had got there before me. Time and time again when I visited someone in need, I would find the Christ awaiting me. On this occasion, I was brought down a peg or two by this lovely old lady who was dying. 'Boy', she said to me (which put me nicely in my place), 'Can we praise God with a few psalms?' Words of love flowed from her lips to the ever-present God. In the next few weeks before she died, I learned that she had been friends with Christ long before I ever arrived on the scene. She truly opened new doors for me. I learned there what I had to learn again and again, that the Christ meets us in the other. Much later I would often ask myself, 'If you cannot accept the otherness of the person you meet, how can you be open to that Great Other which is God?'

This brings to mind the great openness and hospitality that were common to most rural peoples; doors were never closed, strangers were made welcome, meals were shared. Who knew when the Christ would come? Hospitality is the movement away from hostility. Our relationship with others is a mixture, but it is always moving towards enmity or amity, to being open or closed. Too often and too easily we write people off. This is not the way of the Christ who is 'a friend of publicans and sinners'. He is to be met in the other, and if we close the door to another we close it to Him, and we close it on ourselves. This is expressed in the poem from the *Leabhar Breac*, translated by Kuno Meyer:

> O King of the stars!
> Whether my house be dark or bright,
> Never shall it be closed against anyone,
> Lest Christ close His house against me.
> If there be a guest in your house
> And you conceal aught from him,
> 'Tis not the guest that will be without it,
> But Jesus, Mary's Son.[2]

The modern Iona community has a song, 'A Touching Place':

Christ is the world in which we move,
Christ's are the folk we're summoned to love,
Christ's is the voice which calls us to care,
And Christ is the one who meets us there.[3]

We must take seriously the words of Christ: 'As much as you did it to the least of my brothers you did it unto me' (Matthew 25.40). We are not to count only Christians as Christ's brothers and sisters, but all people. Every call to love, every call for help, every call for understanding, is the opening of a door where Christ reaches out. We are able to reach out, to extend ourselves, to be enriched, when we realize that God sets before us each day yet another open door. No matter how restricted we feel, how limited our abilities, God offers us new opportunities and new openings. There is a great danger in seeking to turn back and look for the security and safety of the past, of where we used to be.

Just as life is a battle, it is also a journey, a pilgrimage, a moving on. One of the great curses in life is to become stuck, and unable to move. Once movement stops we begin to die. The Irish monk and missionary Columbanus said that 'Life is not a resting place, life is a road.' It is necessary that we move on, that we accept change, and even the death of the old. Too often we maintain organizations and practices that we should allow to die so that the new may be born. It is amazing how many Christians keep holding on to dead things when they say they believe in the resurrection. We need to make ourselves free and open to the challenges that come before us. Too often we love our cosiness and safety above all things, and shut out anything that would disturb us. We would rather keep our comfortable idols than be confronted by the living God. So we close the door to the other, and to the great Other who is God.

Openness is not to be confined to other people, it is an attitude we must have to all of creation. Anyone who reads their Bible will be aware of how often God has spoken through nature, the burning bush of Moses being a prime example. The early Christians did not see themselves as separate from nature as we seem to, they saw themselves as part of it. God could just as easily speak to them through an animal or through beautiful scenery as He did through another person. This was expressed well by Pelagius writing to an elderly friend:

Look at the animals roaming the forest: God's spirit dwells within them. Look at the birds flying across the sky: God's spirit dwells within them. Look at the tiny insects crawling in the grass: God's spirit dwells within them. There is no creature on earth in whom God is absent. Travel across the ocean to the most distant lands, and you will find God's spirit in the creatures there. Climb up the highest mountain and you will find God's spirit among the creatures who live at the summit. When God pronounced that his creation was good, it was not only that his hand had fashioned every creature; it was that his breath had brought every creature to life. Look too at the great trees of the forest; look at the wild flowers and the grass of the fields; look even at your crops. God's spirit is present within all plants as well. The presence of God's spirit in all living things is what makes them beautiful: and if you look with God's eyes, nothing on earth is ugly.[4]

In our own century, the Jesuit priest Teilhard de Chardin wrote:

> God, in all that is most living and incarnate in him, is not far away from us, altogether apart from the world we see, touch, hear, smell and taste about us. Rather he awaits us every instant in our action, in the work of the moment ... he is at the tip of my pen, my spade, my brush, my needle – of my heart and of my thought.[5]

Before us is a doorway to God. In the book of Revelation the messenger of the Spirit to the church in Philadelphia says, 'This is the message from the one who is holy and true. He has the key that belonged to David and when he opens a door no one can close it, and when he closes it no one can open it ... I have opened a door in front of you ...' (Revelation 3.7, 8). Yet we are always in danger of closing doors so that we can keep to our own ideologies and dogmas. We can even justify our deeds by saying that we want to protect what we have and that others are ignorant.

We have to imagine the reaction in the monastery on Iona. A whole new world was opening up to the Columban mission. Just as Columba himself had made headway with King Brude of Inverness,[6] now they had a chance to make headway with the Angles. Corman's words seemed particularly harsh. He seemed to suggest that these people were not worth the bother, that God could not be interested in them! There was a stunned silence. Heads were bowed in prayer or in shame. No one quite knew what to say. Even the wise abbot Segene was lost for words. Then a quiet but very firm voice spoke out, a monk called Aidan: 'Brother, it seems to me that you were too hard on these untaught minds. You expected too much of them and too soon. You should have followed the example of the apostles, and begun by giving them the milk of simple teaching, gradually instructing them until they were able to accept more.'

Perhaps the door was not closing yet. If Oswald truly wanted a Columban mission, this Aidan could be the man. Like Columba before him he was of a royal household; it was said that he descended from the same race as Bridgit, the abbess and founder of the monastery at Kildare, who died about 525. It is also suggested in the *Martyrology of Donegal* that he was already a bishop of Inis Cathaig, that is the Scattery Islands in the Shannon opposite Kilrush in County Clare. *The Martyrology of Oengus* links Aidan with Cell Mor, the Great Cell of the island of Tiree. Aidan, whose name means 'bright flame', had a heart aflame for God.

Corman must have felt stung by this remark of Aidan. It is all very well to speak out if you have not been there. If he reacted like most of us do, Corman must have said, 'All right, clever one, if you think you can do better why don't you have a go?' Rightly so. It would seem that suddenly all attention was on Aidan. He was a man of discretion and ability. He was known for his gentleness and his absolute dedication. He had just been offered the open door, was he willing to go in? Time would tell whether he was the man to bring the gospel to these barbaric peoples. One thing was for sure, this was an opportunity Aidan did not want to miss; a whole new world was being opened up to him.

'Brother it seems to me that you were too severe.'
Bede 3.5.

1. Learn Psalm 8.1–6:

O Lord our Governor:
    how glorious is your name in all the earth!
Your majesty above the heavens is yet
recounted:
    by the mouths of babes and sucklings.
You have founded a strong defence against
your adversaries:
    to quell the enemy and the avenger.
When I consider these your heavens, the work
of your fingers:
    the moon and the stars which you have set
    in order,
what is man that you should be mindful of
him:
    or the son of man that you should care for
    him?
Yet you have made him little less than a god:
    and crowned him with glory and honour.

If God does that to people, we should be seeking
to respect everyone. Let us seek to discover the
glory of God in the 'other' who comes to us.

2. Think about these words:
'This is the message from the one who is holy
and true. He has the key that belonged to David,
and when he opens a door, no one can close it,

and when he closes it, no one can open it ... I have opened a door in front of you.'
(Revelation 3.7, 8)

What doors are opening for you at this time? What opportunities do you have for reaching out? God is forever expanding our lives and our vision. As long as we live, God presents us with an open door.

3. Leo Tolstoy said, 'Everybody thinks of changing humanity, nobody thinks of changing himself.' Does this apply to you? Are you willing to allow the other person to be themselves or do you demand their transformation? In his book *A Serious Call to a Devout and Holy Life*, William Law says that if we want to be humble like Christ we must 'condescend to all the weaknesses and infirmities of your fellow creatures, cover their frailties, love their excellencies, encourage their virtues, relieve their wants, rejoice in their prosperities, compassionate their distress, receiving their friendship, overlooking their unkindness, forgive their malice, be a servant of servants, and condescend to do the lowest offices to the lowest of mankind.' Do you see yourself fulfilling this ideal?

4. Pray:

> Open my eyes to your presence
> Open my ears to your call
> Open my heart to your love.
> May I open my arms to others
> May I open my heart to strangers
> May I open my door to callers
> That I may be open to you, Lord,
> Open this day and for evermore.

## 3

*Heart Aflame*

Aidan could be just the man to win the kingdom for Christ. Yet at that moment he must have wondered. He had declared what he thought about Corman's mission, and now he was being asked to prove it. Already doubts must have assailed him. Was he up to it? Did he want to leave Iona, and become a pilgrim for the love of God? There was always a danger that he could be killed on the way; that was one kind of martyrdom.

In the Celtic church there were three kinds of martyrdom: red martyrdom was the one everyone knew of, that was the heroic giving of your life-blood for God. Aidan prayed that this would not be required of him – at least until he had fulfilled his mission. Already he was practising the green martyrdom: by prayer and fasting he was disciplining his desires and seeking only the will of God. Green martyrdom was expected of all who dedicated their lives to Christ. If there is no disciplining of our lives, if we give free rein to our desires, we will not become true soldiers of Christ. Green martyrdom is that dying to self that is necessary for fullness of life. Green martyrdom is pruning for growth, it is about extending ourselves.

Now Aidan was to take on board the white martyrdom, though not for the first time. His white martyrdom had begun long ago when he left his home and the people he loved. It began when he left the beautiful and familiar places that were dear to him from his youth. It happened again when he left his bishopric at Inis Cathaig. White martyrdom was the call to leave all and follow Christ, to give up all that was dear to him, to abandon possessions and familiar surroundings for the unknown. White martyrdom was to be freed from place that you might reach outwards and upwards, that you might have the greatest mobility. The rule of Columba said: 'Yield to every rule that is of devotion. Prepare your mind for red martyrdom. Hold your mind steadfast and strong for white martyrdom.' This is only to live out the fact that for all of us life is a road, and we are all moving all the time. In the words of Columbanus, 'Let us concern ourselves with things divine, and as pilgrims ever sigh for and desire our homeland: for the end of the road is ever the object of traveller's hopes and desires, and thus since we are travellers and pilgrims in the world, let us ever ponder on the end of the road, that is of our life, for the end of the roadway is our home.'[1]

The Rule of Columba encouraged its monks to travel lightly through the world: 'Whatsoever, little or much, you possess of anything, whether clothing, food or drink, let it be at the command of the senior and at his disposal. It is not fitting for a religious to have any distinction of property with his brother.'

This does not mean you are not to love your surroundings and the things in it, but it does seek to ensure that you have a right relationship with all around you. No doubt Aidan loved Iona, with its rhythm of prayer and the ebb and flow of its tides. He was very much an island man and a community man. But at least he would take a small group of twelve companions with him – twelve as symbolic of the first disciples. The daunting thought was that Aidan had to be Christ to this group, as he was called to be Christ to everyone whom he met. Other people had to be able to experience the Christ in him and through him. Without him many would not encounter the Christ, many would not know of the Christ. In some strange way Christ was dependent on him. He had to be the Christ to others. But such thoughts could easily lead to megalomania, or the arrogance of the imperial conqueror. To balance this, he had to see Christ in others, in everyone he met. He had to find the Christ in the pagan soldier, in the Anglian palace officials, in those who mocked and scorned Christ. Each person was made by God and loved by God, and the Christ dwelt within them. Aidan was not taking Christ, but meeting Christ. This was a road to adventure and discovery, the great discovery of Christ in the other.

These were fine thoughts, but Aidan knew he would miss Iona. Prayer had been said here for almost seventy years. It was in May 563 that Columba had landed with his twelve disciples. Since that time they had won a rich harvest for Christ in Dalriada and in the land of the Picts. There had been great adventures. There were exciting tales of water dragons being defeated and kingdoms won. The small beginnings on Iona had blossomed into a 'city of God'. It was amazing what the twelve who came with Columba achieved in such a short time. Aidan began to recount their names. There was Baithene, Columba's cousin and foster son, who succeeded him as abbot. Cobthach was Baithene's brother; Ernan was Columba's uncle, and became the superior of the monastery on Hinba. Aidan reeled off the names of the others: Diarmit, who was Columba's close companion, Rus, Fechno, Echoid, Tochannu, Scandal, Grilaan Mochonna and Cairnaan.

Aidan remembered how much Columba had missed Ireland. In fact he had chosen Iona because you could not see Ireland from it. Aidan knew he would not be able to see Iona from where he was going. Two things sprang to his mind. Who would he take with him? Would he ever see Iona again?

During evening prayers, he looked around; so many of these familiar faces were dear to him. They had prayed together and worshipped together day by day. Here were truly some faithful soldiers of Christ. It would be a privilege to have any of them. He would have liked some of the elders, but the journey and the mission could be too much for them. There were some there he would likely never see again; his heart and a prayer went out to them.

After spending time alone in prayer, Aidan decided to look over the island that had been his home for a good while. He walked westwards and southwards till he came to the Port-na-Charaich, Port-of-the-Coracle. It was here that Columba had landed. The sea was raging, though the wind had dropped; great rollers were swinging in from the ocean. Aidan felt secure as he stood on the cliffs and looked westward. He took a long hard look, watching the great white rollers, for he knew his journey would be in the opposite direction. Would he ever see the sun setting in the sea again?

Now he made his way past the waters of Staonaig, to the bright white sands of the bay. Seals were singing as the sun was sinking in the west. It would hurt him to leave this place, but a voice from within was calling him. God had work for him to do elsewhere. He could only say, 'Here am I, Lord, send me.' He started to cross the machair, the sandy pasture with its wild thyme and clover. It is amazing what you are attached to if you love a place. Now he made his way to Dun-I, the hill of Iona. He would climb this and watch the sun go down. How often he had done this and named each island. Looking westwards and towards the north were Tiree and Coll; southwards across the

Sound, there was Colonsay, and the three Paps of Jura looming over the low-lying Islay. To the east was Mull and its great mountain, Ben More. Northwards about eight miles was the island of Staffa with its strange cave, and beyond that Rhum and Eigg, and the blue mountains of Skye in the distance. The sheer splendour of the view reminded Aidan how privileged he was; beauty and peace were all around him, and a feeling of holiness and a deep and lasting divine presence. We have only to look beyond the glory that is about us and we discover the great glory of God. Glory filled the whole place.

The sun had a little while to go before it sank bright red in the west, so Aidan turned to look at the community below. The rath, the defence embankment or vallum that marked out the sacred site, cast long shadows. This rampart of earth and stones was not so much for protection as to mark out the site that had been dedicated to God by fasting and prayer. In a special way the whole site was a holy place, a sanctuary of God. Aidan could pick out what had been Columba's dwelling on the Abb's Tor. On a gentle slope was the church, a scriptorium, the dwelling huts, the refectory and cookhouse, the guesthouse. He could also see a great standing cross and the graveyard. It was quite easy to imagine Columba striding around these wooden buildings to see that all was well.

Outside the vallum there was a fair-sized group of buildings, including a blacksmith's, a carpenter's shop, a kiln for drying corn, two granaries and a mill. Looking at all of this he had many fond memories and realized what a good and balanced life they had. The Rule said for them all: 'There are three labours in the day, prayer, work, reading.

Your own work is to be divided into three parts, your own work and the work of your place, as regards to its real needs: secondly your share in the work of the brethren: lastly to help your neighbours by instruction or writing or sewing garments or whatever labour is required.' Aidan was suddenly aware that he would lose the security of an established community and all its buildings. He would have to start with very little. Strangely, that attracted him. It would be good not to possess anything – though he knew that he would need all sorts of things if he was to do his work properly. Yet if he had a Gospel book, the Psalms and some dedicated men, they would achieve much.

It was now time to watch the sun go down. Tomorrow he would have to decide who would go with him and what talents would be asked of them. The light was fading fast, darkness was sweeping over the island. Soon he would be back in the church for the candle-lighting. Words came to mind, 'Jesus Christ is the light of the world, a light that no darkness can conquer.' He prayed that the Light of Christ would shine upon the eastern shores and that the Angles would accept the Christ. Aidan's heart was aflame with love. He loved the world around him. He loved the work he was being called to do. He loved the feeling of adventure. His heart burned with a great love for the mighty God who called him. He knew why the ancient ones had kept silence; words could not capture his feelings. Who could speak of this great God? He fills all things. Everywhere He is present and invisible; nothing exists without Him. 'This great God will be there wherever I go. I may not know what lies ahead, but I know who is there to meet me.' Aidan's heart flamed with love and he sang:

God there before me
God there behind me
God's love about me
God there above me
God there beneath me
God's strength surround me
God all about me
God deep within me
God's grace toward me.

A strange stillness settled on the island, and on Aidan. He felt that all would be well, that the darkness would give way to light as sure as the sun would rise tomorrow. He prayed that he might be a torch-bearer of the light of Christ.

The next day the men were selected. Some of those who had been with Corman wished to return with Aidan, but this was not thought to be wise. The men chosen would have to be good all-round craftsmen. They would have to be able to build, to cook, to fish and hunt, to milk and farm. They would have to be able to withstand long journeys and deprivations. They would need to be able to stand up to the Anglian warriors, to be men among men, yet they would need to be gentle in their dealings if they were to make progress. A lot was to be expected of these men! Above all they needed to be dedicated men of God who were well balanced in their lives. Aidan had spent much of the night in prayer, asking that he might be the right man for the task, and that his brethren would be able to meet whatever lay ahead. The love of God was about him and his heart was aflame.

Aidan shut himself up with his men in the community church and addressed them: 'My beloved brothers in Christ, co-workers in spiritual conflict, I am consumed with so burning a desire that it drives all other thoughts from my heart. I am resolved, if it be God's will, to go to the land of the Angles and let Christ reveal himself there. Have you anything you want to say on this matter?'

For a short while there was silence, and then they all replied as if with one voice, 'Father, your will is our will, where you go we will go. Have we not left our homeland and our earthly inheritance to put ourselves at your disposal? We will go with you whatever may happen. We seek one thing alone – the will of God.'

Aidan replied, 'God is with us wherever we go. He is our captain and guide, He will shield us and protect us.' A deep silence followed, while each man dedicated himself anew to his Maker.

Aidan was determined that they should travel lightly. It is so easy to clutter up our life with things. Too many possessions make the journey harder and slower. He made sure that what they took was pared down to the bare minimum. He also believed that Oswald would provide them with many of the things that they would later require.

The journey to Bamburgh took many days, and they risked being attacked more than once. Aidan prayed each day for protection and a good journey. The discipline of prayer gave them strength and refreshment on the way. All of the men with him knew the Psalms by heart. Throughout the journey they recited them, the words giving a rhythm to their walking. Psalms were said in rotation from number one to number 150, then they would start again. Yet certain psalms sprang to mind in different places. 'I will lift up my eyes to the hills' was in their hearts and minds even when it was not being said. Now and again a travel-weary heart thought,

'Out of the deep have I called to you, O Lord. Lord hear my voice.' All the Psalms were used to affirm the presence of God who was ever near. Wherever they went, however they felt, God was there with them and before them. In the early morning and in the evening they spent time with the Gospels. Very often it was the Gospel according to St John. Again a book was not used; the scriptures had been learned and were in their hearts and minds. The living word could be contained far better in the heart than on a page. It also meant that whenever they met with anyone, they had the gospel with them and could share it. They loved to quote a text and see if another of the brothers could find a text that was in tune with it. One thought reverberated with another. Nearly all their Bible sessions on the road were times of devotion.

As they approached the kingdom of Oswald, Aidan began to speak to the people in the hill country. They spoke a language much like his own. They were often at least nominally Christian. If they were Christian, they could at least share the gospel and pray a little together. Aidan assumed that Christians liked to pray and wanted to share their faith. There were some language difficulties: but Aidan found apathy or indifference, when he encountered them, far harder to deal with. He also began to realize that within this kingdom of Oswald there was more than one kingdom to win for Christ. The people of the land were of a similar Celtic stock to himself. Rivers, hills and landmarks all had strong Celtic names. It would only take a little practice and he would be able to communicate with the native people. The real difficulty was their fear and resentment of the English. Oswald was a foreigner and an invader. The English were the enemy of occupation, who had driven many of the British off their land and from their homes. Aidan realized that much of his work would be one of reconciliation, the building up of trust and good relationships. His heart went out to these people who were oppressed. He wanted them to know the gospel of liberty and love, also of forgiveness and acceptance. He would have dearly liked to stay among the hill peoples, but his call was to the coast and the fortress of Bamburgh.

At last they came in sight of the eastern sea. It had not appeared until their journey was nearly over. It would be good to get sea air into their lungs again. They were aware that the people they met were now different; these were warrior peoples, even though they were settling in farmsteads. But they were people of culture. Aidan thought some had heard of Christ, but now language was a major difficulty. The brothers were not able to communicate with many people at all. For this reason, when possible, they avoided the little scattered communities and still bore eastwards. The coast was not far away but they travelled on the other side of the hills, making straight for the capital.

When they came to the coast it was to a wide sweeping bay. The tide was out and they could hardly see the sea. There were sea birds a-plenty. Evening prayers were said with a heron fishing nearby. The heron had been one of Columba's favourite birds and it made the little group feel at home. During these last few miles they had seen more people, and the road seemed to be busy with soldiers. They noticed that some of the soldiers were carrying what must have been booty.

One more steep hill, and then a great vista opened up before them. There was a lot of woodland, but much land had been cleared. Directly ahead was a great rock, standing proud in the landscape. Below it was a sprinkling of cottages, and fields with cattle and sheep. On the rock there was a mighty palisade, a fortress truly fit for a king. Beyond it was the sea. Smoke was rising from one or two areas on the high rock. It seemed to be well-fortified, with many inhabitants. As the brothers approached the gates they were stopped by a sentry. They explained who they were, but the language barrier caused difficulty. They repeated the name 'Oswald' more than once, and 'Iona' again and again. But the guards did not understand enough to make any headway. Then one guard left and returned with a tall, slim regal-looking man with a short, pointed beard. Aidan's heart leaped. Surely this was Oswald himself. The king had come out to meet them. Recognizing their attire, Oswald welcomed them in their own tongue. He issued an order to the guards which Aidan and his followers did not understand, but they were ushered in quickly.

Oswald wanted to know about their journey. He asked for news of Iona and Abbot Segene. He mentioned other names, only some of which were familiar. Soon they were offered a place to rest and a meal to refresh them. This king was in no way barbaric, though he was obviously a mighty warrior. All around were battle-shields and spears, great swords and bows. There were animal skins on the floor and a great fire burning. The meal was more than they would normally eat but today was special. For a while Aidan felt nervous, but he realized Oswald was personally determined to make them feel at home.

Soon they were talking over a campaign of teaching. Oswald was anxious that his closest subjects should be educated. If the kingdom was to grow it had to be built on more than a foundation of conquest. A school was of the utmost importance. He knew they would need a church. He understood that they would want to deal with the British also. In all this he was willing to give them whatever resources they needed. He kept emphasizing the importance of getting started. Never once did he mention Corman. Oswald insisted that the brothers remained in the most comfortable part of his palace and that they allowed themselves to be looked after by his servants. Aidan was about to object, then realized that this could be a good way of making contact with these Angles, and beginning to learn how to communicate with them. There was certainly some interest shown when they said their prayers at night and again in the early morning. The monks did not make a show of their devotions, but they made sure that their hosts knew what they were doing.

Over the next few days Oswald proved that he was true to his word. His generosity knew no bounds. If Aidan or his men needed anything Oswald supplied it. In fact they had to be careful in stating their needs, for Oswald seemed to be able to produce most things almost immediately. He made sure they had space for their worship, giving them a room to be set aside as sacred for the purpose. He offered them the full use of the palace. More than this, he gave them much of his time. He was also ready to come to worship with them. Sometimes they would find he had been the first to enter their little sanctuary and was sitting with his hands open and upturned and resting on his knees, his eyes closed, and praying. They were to discover that this was the posture that Oswald most often took up for his prayers. In the early days Oswald himself acted as an interpreter for them when he was able. When other duties prevented him, he delegated the task to one of the thanes who had been with him in Dalriada. Aidan was thrilled to discover that a few of the leading men at the palace could speak his language and were willing to help him learn their native tongue.

Oswald would have liked the school to have been in Bamburgh. He waved his arms and said, 'You can have any land you like to build your monastery on.' At this Aidan was silent, and could not answer. He knew that if he was in the shadow of the royal residence, many of the British would find this offensive, or would be afraid to come. Another difficulty was all the activity that was going on around the palace. It was far too busy a place for them to establish themselves. Aidan said he would talk it over with his brothers. He knew that they would have to decide quickly, or Oswald might think they did not appreciate his offer. Not one of them wanted the protection of the palace. They realized that it would not be good either for their mission or their development. They needed to distance themselves a little from the king.

When Oswald was told this, he frowned a little but was his usual generous self. They could have anywhere in his kingdom. They could go to one of the great towns, they could have some of the wonderful rolling hill country, they could have a settlement by one of the rivers. The kingdom was large and it was at their disposal.

What Aidan did next Oswald found hard to understand. He looked out to sea and pointed to some islands not far from the fortress. 'How large are those?' Some of his companions, missing their island home, thrilled at the question.

'Not large enough nor productive enough for you to do your work on them,' came a rather blunt reply.

'What, none of them?' Aidan asked in disappointment.

'Well there is one, if you can call it an island,' said Oswald as he turned northwards and pointed. 'It is the farthest one away from here. It is larger than the rest. It has its own water supply, which the others do not have. There is much hazel growing there that could be used in building. But it is not a proper island.'

Those listening to Oswald wondered how an island could not be an island. Seeing their look of puzzlement, he explained. 'The land is not so far from the shore as the other islands. In fact when the tide recedes it is not an island but part of the mainland. Each day it is cut off by the tides, and each day it becomes open again. You can cross to the mainland when the tide is out, on horseback or on foot. But when the tide is high you can only get off the island by boat, and there are some very strange sea currents that run about the island.'

'What is its name?' asked Aidan.

'I believe it is called Inis Metcaud' replied Oswald, 'and I have been told it means the "Island of the strong winds".'

'It sounds as if we may have found our new

home,' replied Aidan. Then to Oswald, 'If you do not mind, it seems it could be just the sort of place we are looking for. It is not far from your royal dwelling and yet it will give us the silence and the separation we feel we need.'

Oswald still seemed doubtful, but thinking that maybe these island monks would be more at home with the sea around them, he agreed, and said, 'The island is yours.'

Aidan turned to his monks: 'It appears we are on the road again. We will move off in the morning.'

### EXERCISES

'His life is in marked contrast to the apathy of our own times, for all who accompanied him, whether monks or layfolk, were required to meditate, that is either to read the scriptures or learn the Psalms.' Bede 3.5

1. Psalm 139.1–9. Recite these words slowly, thinking of Aidan, then again thinking of how they apply to you.

O Lord, you have searched me out and known me:
    you know when I sit or when I stand
    you comprehend my thoughts long before.
You discern my path and the places where I rest:
    you are acquainted with all my ways.

For there is not a word on my tongue:
    but you, Lord, know it altogether.
You have encompassed me behind and before:
    and have laid your hand upon me.
Such knowledge is too wonderful for me:
    so high that I cannot endure it.
Where shall I go from your spirit:
    or where shall I flee from your presence?
If I ascend into heaven you are there:
    if I make my bed in the grave you are there
    also.
If I spread out my wings towards the morning:
    or dwell in the uttermost parts of the sea,
even there your hand shall lead me:
    and your right hand shall hold me.

2. Read Isaiah 6.1–8.

The 5p exercise is a good way to meditate upon the Scriptures. I call it 5p because each section begins with the letter 'P' – PAUSE, PRESENCE, PICTURE, PONDER, PROMISE

PAUSE

Stop all that you are doing, and relax. Still your body and your mind. Gently seek to relieve all points of tension in your body. Make sure you are sitting comfortably. Put any anxious thoughts out of your mind. If necessary, fill it steadily and slowly with the word 'Peace'. Seek to be at peace in yourself.

PRESENCE

Know that you are in God's presence. Say, 'You encompass me, behind and before, and have laid your hand on me.' Remind yourself that you are in the heart of God. Nothing can separate you from the love of God in Christ Jesus. You dwell in Him and He in you. Take time, and remind yourself of this reality.

PICTURE

Picture Isaiah in the throne room. *The king is dead and the throne is empty.* Isaiah has lost his support with Uzziah's death. He has lost his security. The future looks bleak. *The king is dead and the throne is empty.* All is now unsure. Chaos could easily descend, the way ahead looks black. *The king is dead and the throne is empty.* There is no hope, no joy; all could soon come to an end. *The throne is* . . . 'I saw the Lord. He was sitting on his throne . . .' Into the emptiness comes a great vision. The Lord, high and exalted, is on his throne. Isaiah bows low, he only gets a glimpse of glory, the very edge of God's robes. The throne is not empty, the world is not empty. The divine presence is all about us. 'Holy, holy, holy! The Lord Almighty is holy! His glory fills the world.'

Picture what this means for you! God's glory is all about you. How unworthy Isaiah felt – as anyone must who comes close to God. 'Lord, I am not worthy.' But those whom God calls, God prepares. Hear the words, 'Your guilt is gone, and your sins are forgiven', and let them work in you. Then the voice, 'Whom shall I send? Who will be our messenger? Hear and know that He speaks to you. For all who are called, for all whose hearts are aflame, there is only one true answer: 'I will go, send me!'

PONDER

God calls each of us in our own way. God calls you. Have you heeded the still small voice? Are you sensitive to His call? Do you prefer not to listen? What does God ask of you? Are you ready to say, 'I will go! Send me!'?

**PROMISE**

This week you will set aside time to be quiet, to be aware. Promise to relax in God's presence and to seek His will. Say quietly and regularly, 'I will go, Lord! Send me!'

3. Pray:

> Lord God of the Universe,
> Touch my eyes that I may see you
> Touch my lips that I may praise you
> Touch my heart that I may love you
> Touch my mind that I may know you
> Touch my life that I may glorify you
> And send me out to do your will.

## 4

*Preparing the Ground*

The island was larger than Aidan had expected, though he was not quite sure where it began. Some of it was great sand dunes. The main part of the island seemed to be at its southern end. It felt about the size of Iona, though there was no hill like Dun-I. Two rocky outcrops, exposed to the sea, made the only hills on the island, on the north-eastern shore there were some caves. It was near these caves he heard the seals singing and it reminded him of Iona. God had blessed him and his companions with a good land. There was much hazel wood and a quantity of stunted trees, more trees than on Iona. But the trees had to survive the winds and the salt spray. In the sea there were ducks and many gulls, there were mussels, oysters and winkles. The seals suggested there were fish in abundance. There was a good deal of machair that would be ideal for pasture for their cattle. Cattle were essential to the community, not only for meat and milk, but for providing skins for parchment for the making of books. The soil was light and sandy, no doubt it would be good for growing grain. There was a small freshwater lough that reminded Aidan again of Iona. His heart was nearly bursting for joy. God had truly brought him into a good and pleasant land.

From the southern end of the island Aidan could see the smoke rising at Bamburgh. He could see the great rock on which the fortress stood. The king was near at hand. Here on the island Aidan could follow the Rule of Columba which said, 'Be alone in a separate place near a chief city, if your conscience is not prepared to be in common with the crowd.' Here they were far enough away from the palace to be free from its own activity and demands, yet near enough to be of use to the king and the leaders of the people. Here you could feel the silence. Here would be a place of solitude, stillness and sanctity, essentials for growth in the Spirit. There is need for us all to get away from the business of life and stand at the edge of things. Yes, the island would be their home.

There was a great deal to do. Land had to be cleared, and a vallum built. There was need for a church, though a standing cross of wood could serve for a while, until they could put up a building and a stone cross. Each of the brothers needed a cell as a place of retreat and for shelter. The farm needed to be in action as soon as possible. Then the primary reasons for which they came: they would have to start a school, and they would need to reach out in mission to the people of the land, both the English and the British.

It was important at this stage to get their priorities right. There was so much to do that they had to decide carefully and lay a firm foundation. So a course of action was decided on, one that amazed the king when he heard of it. No land would be cleared, nothing done, until they had hallowed the land and cast out any evil. The area for the monastic community within the vallum was marked out and then the next forty days were a time of prayer and fasting. The brothers had to be sure of their priority, and let others see it. Their priority was to give themselves in adoration to God; everything else could wait. It was only by doing this that they could enrich the lives of those who came to them. It was no use talking *about* God if they did not talk *to* Him. God was not a theory to be handed on to others, He is a person to be met and His presence enjoyed. Here the love of God was to burn within them. They did not try to make this happen, for it was a fact: they tried to become more aware of the reality that 'we dwell in Him and He in us'.

The period set aside for this preparation was forty days. As our Lord spent forty days in the wilderness, Aidan and his brothers spent forty days in prayer and fasting. As Jesus spent the time sorting out His priorities and putting His faith in the Father, so these men from Iona wrestled with their future. It was a time of depth, dedication and discipline, not of impoverishment but of enrichment, extension and vision. Without this awareness their world would be destroyed: we need to know the great mysteries that are about us, and within us.

More than this, here was land to win back for God. Here on this island was a desire for Paradise regained. From the land within the enclosure all violence would be excluded, along with all demons and darkness. All hostile elements had to be banished, this has to be a place to reveal the presence, the power and the peace of God. Standing near the wooden cross which they had erected, Aidan began the cleansing of the site by prayer. He prayed to the God of the seven directions and sought his blessing. He looked eastwards over the land to the sea, praying in the direction of the rising sun.

> Praise God for daylight
> Praise God for sunlight
> Praise God for Christ light
> Praise God for our rising to life today
> Praise God who keeps us in life.
> Bless all that comes to us from the east
> Bless all that comes in from the sea.
> May they find peace in this holy place.

Time was spent in silence, each brother adding power to the prayer, each letting it fill his heart: 'May this be a holy place, a place of peace. Let the place be one of beauty that protects us, a place that is a joy to the eyes. A place where heaven and earth are one.'

Now, following the direction of the sun, Aidan looked southwards in the direction of Bamburgh and the royal palace. They could not see the palace from where they stood because of the hill they called the Heugh, but they knew it was not far away.

Blessed be God of noonday
Blessed be God of this day
Blessed be God of each day
Blessed be God for the powers he gives us
    today.
Bless all who come to us from the south
Bless all who come from battle seeking peace
Bless all who flee from terror seeking hope
Bless all who flee from darkness seeking light.
May they find refreshment in this holy place.

Each man tried to picture some of the people at the palace, not only Oswald and the leaders but servants and slaves. They prayed that all peoples might know the liberty and joy of the children of God.

Aidan now turned to face the west. Briefly his thoughts went to Ireland and his home, then on to Iona. He was delighted that he could still see the sun set over the sea, that is, if the tide was in and covering the tidal flats.

Blessed be God of the evening
Blessed be God in the gloaming

Blessed be God in the darkness
Blessed be God in the night
Blessed be God in the ebb tide
Blessed be God in our weakness
Blessed be God in our doubt.
Protect us from the darkness
Protect us from all evil
Protect us from the demons
Protect us from all wickedness.
May we find shelter in this holy place.

The brothers were used to thinking about the battles they were waging against the evil powers. They were aware that there are many forces of darkness ready to engulf us and imprison us. There are many demons that would destroy us. Each prayed for protection and made the sign of the cross. Each asked that God would shield and guard them. Here was a battle to be fought, every bit as real as the battle that Oswald had fought at Heavenfield. If we make light of the battle it is because we have already given in to the enemy or have become insensitive to what is around us. They prayed to the Lord, that they might be alert to all that would diminish and destroy them, that He would be their strength.

Aidan now turned to the north, to the area of darkness and the unknown.

Blessed be God in the unknown
Blessed be God in our doubts
Blessed be God giving light in the darkness.
Protect all who are assailed in their faith
Protect all who are mocked and scorned
Protect all who are persecuted by others.
Make this place a hiding place for them

Make this place a place of healing
Make this place a place of renewal
Make this place a place where we rise again.

Many a thought went out for the British who had lost their land, who had been driven from their homes. Even this island had seen the betrayal and death of the mighty British king Urien ap Rheged. Here this Christian king, half a century before Aidan arrived, had been murdered by Morcant, one of his own supporters, whilst he tried to drive out the English. Quietly they remembered all who had given their lives in the service of others.

The circle was completed, the area within the vallum dedicated. But there were still three directions to be acknowledged as God's own. Aidan now bent low and touched the earth:

Blessed be the Creator of the earth
Blessed be the Lord of the harvest
Blessed be the Christ who descended
Blessed be the Word made flesh.
Bless to us the land that it may be fruitful
Bless to us the ground that it may yield a
    harvest
Bless to us the earth that it may be the place of
    our resurrection.

All who heard rejoiced at these last words. Here Aidan hoped to stay and grow. Here he hoped to remain, yet change. Here he wanted to die and to rise again. 'Blessed be the God who descended into hell. Protect us, Lord, from the evil one. Blessed be the Lord who rose again with the dust of the earth clinging to Him.'

All this time Aidan had been bowed low, his hands on the ground. Now with face aglow he seemed to rise from the depths. His face looked upwards, skywards. His face seemed to shine with joy. He raised his arms until his hands were above his head:

> Blessed be the God who lifts us up
> Blessed be the God of heaven
> Blessed be the risen and ascended Lord
> Blessed be the Christ in glory.
> Bless us, Lord, with vision
> Bless us, Lord, with faith
> Bless us, Lord, with hope.
> May this place be a sacred place
> May this be where heaven and earth meet.
> Amen. Amen.

There was a resounding 'Amen' from all the brothers. Aidan, almost unaware, remained in prayer, with hands raised, not stretched out in cross-vigil but uplifted in adoration of the God of all directions – the God in front, behind, on right and left, the God above and the God below. The act of enclosure was complete. We dwell in Him. In Him we live and move and have our being. Nothing can separate us from the love of God. Each man was silent for a long time, abiding in the presence, returning to a lost Eden, worshipping their Maker, Redeemer and Sustainer and abiding in the love of the Three.

The last direction was inward. After a long silence, with only the sound of the waves, Aidan lowered his hands and touched his head:

> God is within
> God in my head and in my thinking
> God in my eyes and in my seeing
> God in my mouth and in my speaking
> God in my heart and in my loving

God in my hands and in each action
God in my feet and on each journey
God within me and without me
God in the heart of friend and stranger
God in the other who comes to me.

Each person had to respect all who came into this holy place for with them came the Christ. The Christ in me, meets the Christ in you. This would be expressed yet again in the Common Union, that 'we are the body of Christ'. Aidan's heart was aflame with love for God, for creation, and for his fellow-beings.

For the next forty days, silence was stronger than words, stillness more powerful than actions. Forty days of prayer and fasting was a witness to what they were about. The ground had to be prepared, like any ground that is to be freed of weeds and bear a crop. But there was no way they could proclaim the love of God if they themselves did not enjoy His presence. Let no one be mistaken, this was work, and often hard work. Like all living relationships, it was ever moving and changing, and had to be worked at if it was to last and to be enjoyed.

During this time they fasted every day until the evening, except on Sundays which were always days of celebration. Even when they broke their fast they took only a morsel of bread, an egg and a little watered milk. This they accepted as part of their Rule, the proper and disciplined way to dedicate a site through prayer and fasting.

After the forty days it was time to build. The earth bank was made, to show clearly the holy place. It enclosed not just the church but the whole site. Not only would prayer be offered to God.

They would offer their labour, their sweat and their tears. They would offer prayer, but in much the same way they would offer the tilling of the ground, the milking of cows, the catching of fish and the teaching of young men. All work was sacred, for all was done in God's presence and to His glory. The sawing of wood and the fixing of timbers were as much acts of worship as kneeling before the altar. There was no false division into sacred and secular. Hands that were already toughened became calloused with so much hard labour, but it gave them so much joy. The work-worn hands were the same hands that raised the chalice in the Eucharist. Love gave them energy. Yet all would be glad to have a break from digging and moving stones. They worked until they could work no more, either through bodily weariness, hunger or darkness, then they went to their learning and reading, and then to their prayers. The Rule of Columba said, 'The measure of your work shall be until the tears come, until your perspiration comes often. The measure of your prayers shall be until the tears come.' There was no doubt in their mind that whatever we offer to God has truly to be costly to ourselves; half-hearted efforts are not true acts of praise and worship.

The church building was a simple affair made from oak planks and beams brought in from the mainland. The roof was thatched with bents, wiry grasses from the sand dunes. Following the tradition of Columba, they built their church of oak rather than of stone. Perhaps it was to express that we have no abiding city, that building on earth is not eternal. Probably also it was to keep that strange link with their distant past; the oak had been a sacred tree to the Celts and was still very special. Of all the trees it was the most strong and lasting. The church was barn-like in its simplicity, yet here on the sacred site it was an extra-sacred place, a reminder that all is dedicated to God and belongs to Him. It was yet another fixing of a place to remind people that heaven and earth are not separate but one. Here God could be met and worshipped.

Huts were soon built as cells. Upright poles of birch were driven into the ground less than two feet apart, and a second line was built in parallel about a foot away from the first, to form the outline of the walling. Pliable hazel and willow branches were woven into hurdles, and tied to the inner and outer poles. Once this was done, panniers of earth were poured into the gap to make a solid infilling. The inner and outer walls were smeared with clay, or daub. During the weaving of the saplings the brethren would pray quietly. Often not a word would be heard for hours, each meditating and weaving into his life the power and the presence of God. How often, again and again, this weaving pattern appeared in Celtic art. It was the basis of their house building, of their clothes, and of their prayers. Heaven and earth, God and each person are interwoven. God made it so, that we are woven together with Him and with each other. God and each individual are interdependent, remove one piece and all are affected. If one piece is missing the whole structure suffers. Often, whilst weaving hurdles, the brethren chanted, a music not so much concerned with words but vibrant with memories of hymns and psalms. The sound of their chanting was very like the rising and falling sound of the sea. They all knew what depths were in this sound, though to a stranger it might have sounded just like the hum of bees.

Oswald had offered help, as he wanted the school immediately. But Aidan had refused this initial assistance. The preparation could not be done by people who were not committed. They were not just building houses, they were building a kingdom. They were not just clearing the land of weeds, but cleansing it of its past, and getting rid of anything that would destroy the sacredness of the place. Such work could not be done by pagan soldiers. Aidan explained this, but agreed to accept help at the next stage. He would need a herd of cows, he would need barns, he would need grain to sow. Tools were needed, and raw materials. They would also have to have a boat or two, one for fishing and another for journeying out to meet others. Later they would build their own craft, but a gift of boats at this early stage would speed their mission. They would also need one or two horses for speedy travel when necessary. Oswald was eager to supply whatever they needed, in the hope that the school could start soon.

Once the cells were built, the brothers were ready to take on the first pupils. As there were twelve brothers, there would be twelve pupils to start with. Each pupil would have a teacher, an *anamchara*, that is one who shared his cell. Not all teaching would be done one-to-one but each needed a personal guide and soul mate. The foundations had been laid, now the work Oswald had called them to do could begin.

'The man of God wished first of all to purify the site of the monastery from the taint of earlier crimes by prayer and fasting, and make it acceptable to God before the laying of the foundations.' Bede 3.23[1]

1. Psalm 1 (Are we truly seeking the way of the Lord? Do we dedicate ourselves to this with joy?)

Blessed is the man who has not walked in the counsel of the ungodly:
    nor followed the way of sinners,
    nor taken his seat amongst the scornful.
But his delight is in the law of the Lord:
    and on that law will he ponder day and night.
He is like a tree planted beside streams of water:
    that yields its fruit in due season.
Its leaves also shall not wither:
    and look, whatever he does it shall prosper.
As for the ungodly, it is not so with them:
    they are like the chaff which the wind scatters.
Therefore the ungodly shall not stand up at the judgement:
    nor sinners in the congregation of the righteous.
For the Lord cares for the way of the righteous:
    but the way of the ungodly shall perish.

2. Read Luke 6.46–9
Use the 5p exercise: PAUSE, PRESENCE, PICTURE, PONDER, PROMISE.

PAUSE
Stop your busyness. Take time out to know that the

world can go on without you. Be still. Tell your body to be at peace. Tell your mind to be at peace. Tell your emotions to be at peace. Tell your spirit to be at peace. Accept the stillness and the quiet that God gives to you. Accept the deep peace that He offers you. If the mind wants to wander, repeat 'Peace' each time it strays and bring it back. Rest in the peace that only God can give.

PRESENCE
Be aware that God never leaves you. If you rely on your emotions, your mind can tell you lies! God is here, whatever you feel. God is with you even if you cannot feel or know it. You may like to use a prayer to quietly reflect this reality; if so use the prayer at the end of these exercises.

PICTURE
Seek to visualize the story of the two builders. The man who dug out foundations until he reached the rock would take a good deal of time. For a long time there was no apparent building up, only the laying of foundations. The other man would have quick results; his house would go up in no time. He would pour scorn on the man who wanted foundations. He would take it easy when the other was still building. He could rest and play when the other needed to settle himself on the rock. When the houses were finished they both looked alike. No one could see the foundations, though even in small squalls the firmness of one showed whilst the other trembled. When the real storms came, one totally collapsed and the other stood firm. Look and see, one has been swept away and the other remains.

PONDER

What are you building on? What are the foundations of your life? How enduring are they? Fortunately we can underpin our house at any time. We can strengthen our foundations. It is no use putting it off until another day, we do not know what storms will come or when. Again we need to learn to 'be strong in the Lord and in the power of His might.' Are you truly building for the future, a future that should be eternal?

PROMISE

That every day you will lay foundations, starting each day rejoicing in the presence and power of God.

That you will regularly review your life and make sure that the foundations are secure.

3. Pray the prayer of seven directions, giving depth to each direction yourself.

> God ever before me
> God protecting behind me
> God strength on my right
> God power on my left
> God supporting beneath me
> God uplifting above me
> God in love enfolding me
> God within and about me
> God with me always.

## 5

## *The Glorious Liberty*

Aidan often looked back and wondered how his life might have been. He could have been a rich man with all sorts of possessions. Like Columba, he came from a ruling family, and could have owned many things. He could have built up a store of gold and increased his lands. But he had no longing in that direction, no desire for possessions. He had seen rich men fight to keep goods that they must leave one day. He had seen men die for very poor bits of land. He knew some who were afraid to leave their premises in case they were robbed. He knew others who lay awake at night fearing they might lose what they had gained. It would seem that most people believed that the more you have the better off you are. Aidan knew it was not so. He had discovered the great freedom of being dis-possessed. He had also discovered that the most generous of people were often those who had very little. Many times, in the hill country, the poorest of people would offer him far more than an equal portion of their food. He was beginning to learn that it was truly blessed to be poor in spirit, and it is more blessed to give than to receive.

This learning about poverty had begun when he first entered a monastery. He had to leave so much behind. Not only things, but also his wilfulness and his desire to command. When he left Ireland for Iona, he knew he was leaving his own tribe and people. He was leaving behind a certain security and respect. He had had servants who would obey his least command. Now, he knew he had less than some of his former servants. This knowledge was enforced when he heard the Rule of Columba: 'Be always naked in the imitation of Christ and the Evangelists. Whatsoever, little or much, that you possess of anything, whether clothing, food or drink, let it be at the command of the senior and at his disposal, for it is not befitting for a religious to have any distinction of property with his own free brother.'

Aidan learned to do without things. He had nothing that he called his own. He would give up, or give away, anything he had, if so required. He would leave where he was at the command of his superior and go wherever he was ordered. Slowly but surely he learned to travel lightly. He discovered that there is very little you really need for journeying. He also knew that the less you had the less you need fear being robbed. The more you carried about with you the more anxious and burdened you became. He came to know that the truly rich were not the ones with the most possessions but the people who were able to give away what they had. The others did not have possessions, they were possessed, captured, by the very things they thought they owned. Time and time again the words of Jesus came to mind, 'What does it profit a man to win the whole world and lose his own soul?' or 'What can a man give in exchange for his soul?' Too many people were growing rich at the expense of their own well-being. A good way of life was often lost by ever seeking more. So Aidan rejoiced whenever he saw a generous act. Likewise he was sad when he saw a person selling themselves just to acquire more. Contentment is truly a divine gift.

The king, though determined to keep his kingdom, was a generous man. Aidan watched Oswald at prayer. The king sat; perhaps it was hard for him to kneel, maybe he was afraid of what some of his less Christian courtiers would think. Aidan wished he would kneel more often. But he stayed seated a long time in meditation and prayer. Often he would be found in church in the early hours. He said that the early morning was his only time to escape from the business of his kingdom and concentrate on the kingdom of God. Like the monks, he needed space, solace, solitude and silence, so that his prayers and awareness of God could deepen.

Oswald always placed his hands upon his knees with the palms open and upwards. They were not grasping hands, they were generous open hands. He had given the monastery much and had ensured that they survived the early days. The same open hands often gave away to the poor. He had appointed one of his servants to attend to the poor and make sure they were not ignored or sent away empty. He had often been told that Christ said, 'As you do it to the least of these, you do it to me.' He tried to remember this when confronted with the poor. Whilst at Iona he had heard the story of another soldier called Martin. He could almost remember the voice that told him the story.

At a certain time when Martin had nothing except his sword and his military uniform, he went out on a cold winter's night when the weather was severe. At the gates of the city of Amiens he met a poor man begging. All were passing by and taking no notice. There were plenty of beggars about. Martin decided that if all the others were ignoring this man, he must come to his aid. Yet what could he do? He had already given away many of the things he once had. He had no money and nothing he could easily give the man. Then, taking his sword, he divided his cloak into two equal parts. He gave one part to the beggar and wrapped himself in the other. People passing by and fellow-soldiers laughed at Martin, though some felt ashamed that they had not helped. Some of them could easily have clothed the beggar without exposing themselves to the cold, or to ridicule. Martin's act was one of true generosity and love. It was that night that Martin had a vision of Christ. The Saviour was arrayed in half a cloak and saying to the angels, 'Martin, who is still a catechumen, clothed me with this robe.' Oswald had seen the beautiful book that contained this story in the library on Iona, and it had been an elderly monk who had related it to him.

Oswald the soldier tried to live by this high ideal. He could not be a monk, that was not his calling. But he could be open-handed. There was a certain Easter when Aidan had gone to Bamburgh to dine at the palace. Normally when he went he still ate frugally and escaped from the feasting hall as soon as was possible. He and his brothers would seek to get away from the noise to pray in quiet. On this occasion, being a special festival, the best of food was served up, on a silver dish. As the meal was about to begin, and a blessing was being asked upon it, a nervous-looking servant appeared in the doorway. He told the king that there was a great company of poor people gathering outside. The winter had been hard and they were starving. The meagre resources that they lived on had not lasted through the lean times. Oswald stood up immediately, pointing to the silver dish in front of him, which was laden with food. 'Take this out to them, and see that they all get something to eat.' He paused slightly and then continued, 'And give them the silver dish that the food is on. See that it is divided up among them so that they all have something for another day.' The servant did not know what to say. He bowed low and then walked out with the great silver dish and its contents being carried by two other serving men. Aidan was deeply moved by such generosity. Taking hold of the open hand of Oswald he said, 'May this hand never wither with age.' Here was a king who was generous indeed. Aidan prayed that many others would follow his noble example.

Gifts poured into the monastery, not only money but horses, cattle, land, ploughs, boats, gifts for the church and for the building of other churches. Aidan did not mind this as long as the brothers did not set their heart on these things. They were simply tools for furthering the kingdom of God. Aidan was delighted that so much was being made possible. Other churches and monasteries were being built. Up and down the coast, and inland, little churches were built or repaired, as staging posts on their walking mission. People were being taught the faith and leaders of the kingdom were being influenced by what the monks were teaching them. Money and possessions are good if you can use them for the benefit of others. Nothing was meant to be hoarded, all was meant to be shared and held in common.

If Aidan was given more than he felt they could use, he gave it away to the poor. As God had freely given, so he gave it away. There was no loss in this but a great gain. All the countryside around was talking of the generosity of the monks of the island. Many came for help and no one really in need went away empty. What amazed some of the visitors was that the monks kept so little for themselves and ate so frugally. These men lived like the early disciples and their lives showed the power of the gospel. Truly they lived by what they taught.

Once in a while Aidan would go to the local market where slaves were being sold. The first time he bought one it amazed the onlookers. He was a man of some standing, he had a right to have a few slaves if he desired, and there was no doubt they would be well looked after. But somehow they did not expect it of Aidan. Aidan had paid the price asked for him. Some even said he had paid more than the going rate. True, the man was a valuable slave and could be useful. They were more amazed still when they heard that Aidan had set the man free. The tale continued, for the free man decided he did not want to leave Aidan or the community. Where could he go? What could he do? It was then Aidan offered him a place in the school and the opportunity to train with the others to be a priest.

People were talking about this school where members of the royal family and slaves shared in the learning. In the schooling there was no distinction. Aidan hoped they would learn more about true freedom, whether they were freed, slave or courtier. Aidan himself lived as the poorest of the brothers. He continued to follow the teachings of Columba: 'Follow almsgiving above all things. Take no food until you are hungry. Sleep not until you are weary. Speak not except you are on business. Every increase which comes to you in lawful meals, or in wearing apparel, give it for pity to the brethren that want it, or to the poor in like manner.' Time and time again Aidan's heart sang for joy as he gave away what had been given to him. He thrilled to see the pleasure that others showed from receiving gifts that he did not need. He remembered the story of St Lawrence, one of the early martyrs in Rome, who had not only given away all he had, he gave his life in witness to his faith.

Lawrence was Archdeacon of Rome during the

persecution of Valerian in the third century. He saw the execution of his bishop, Sixtus. Lawrence, as keeper of the treasures of the church, was ordered by the authorities to produce its treasures. He asked for a day to be able to collect them all together. He spent that day among the poorest of the city giving them all he could. The next day he appeared at the tribunal with a great crowd of the city's poor and disabled. When asked to produce the treasures of the church, Lawrence declared as he pointed to the poor, 'These are the treasures of the church.'

Aidan wanted to live like this. He wanted the church to be rich in people. Even then he was not concerned with mere numbers, he was only anxious that all should have the opportunity of the riches of the gospel. Often he left the island monastery to walk into the hills. There was a little church out at Gefrin by the river Glen. Sometimes he would use that as his base and move out from there. He would seek out small communities and strive to minister to them. He carried little apart from what was in his heart and mind. He was touched by the generosity of the hill people. They were not hostile to strangers, even though his approach might have caused anxiety. They were always willing to share what they had with him. On Wednesdays and Fridays, Aidan surprised them by refusing food until three in the afternoon. For him these were fast days, and on these days he never ate until after the hour Christ died upon the cross.

Aidan's attitude to food was like his attitude to possessions, there was no need to have more than you really required. He noticed, more than once, that some people needed to cram themselves with as much as possible. In the palace he saw that this often applied to the soldiers and how much they drank. What worried him was not so much the amounts but that it spoke of unrest and an emptiness within. Aidan was sure that the more you poured out for God, the more you were filled with well-being. The more you gave away, the more room there was for God to enter. Time and time again he would go to his favourite Gospel, St John, and say to himself or others, 'God so loved the world that he gave, and giving is an expression of the love of God. It is God who gives us life. God gives us love. God gives us of His very self. Giving is of the essence of God. In giving we share in the love of the Divine.'

Students were taught not only to give of things but to give of themselves. The teaching was clear: If you give of things you give little, but if you give of yourself you give all that you have. Give yourself wholly to what you do. Give your undivided attention to each act, for this is the way to wholeness. Whatever asks you for your action or attention, let it be whole-hearted. A divided self is of the devil. No matter how menial the task, let it be done to the glory of God, and it will be transformed. But you cannot do it to His glory if you are unwilling to give of your best, of your whole self. Do not think that some tasks are beneath you, for that is the way of pride. Learn to do even the lowliest of tasks as it is a way of improving our world and bringing in the kingdom of God.

Aidan did not just seek open hands, but open eyes, open ears, open hearts. Eyes had to become open enough to see beyond the obvious. Vision had to be extended until it saw into the very depths of creation, until it was dazzled with the glory of the divine Presence which underlies all. There were too many people who were blind to the Presence. There were too many who preferred not to see the needs of others. It is amazing how convenient it is for some to be blind. Ears had to be tuned to hear what was not said but only hinted at. Ears had to be open to the God who speaks through his world and through other people. There had to be an openness and a receptivity to all that comes towards us. Silence, stillness and solitude are essential in the training of openness. The ears have to be tuned to hear the 'still small voice'. Time and again the words from the Psalm were used: 'Be still, and know that I am God.'

The heart, if hostile towards people or events, is capable of great destruction. The heart has to be hospitable, welcoming, open. A heart that is open is life-giving and life-enhancing. We must learn to accept, and to forgive. We must reach out in love as God loves us. Plenty of food in a house of hatred is not sustaining. Love makes up for the lack of many things. Know that you are loved and accepted and let that be mirrored in your loving.

Such words often passed through Aidan's mind. When alone he would act out the greatest deed of giving, standing with his feet together and his arms outstretched in cross-vigil. He looked at his shadow and saw the clear shape of the cross. 'God so loved the world that he gave.' Aidan would sometimes stay in this position, speaking no words, until he could bear it no longer, until his arms ached and the tears came. He was always amazed at the people who wanted to shine brightly for God but who were afraid of being burned. Sometimes he would pray tracing the wounds of Christ:

I give my mind to you, Lord,
I give my mind to you.
I give my heart to you, Lord,
I give my heart to you.
I give my hands to you, Lord,
I give my hands to you.
I give my feet to you, Lord,
I give my feet to you.

His students were encouraged to ask God to open them up and use them for His glory. Short sentences could be used, with long silences between them:

Lord, open my eyes to your presence . . .
Lord, open my ears to your call . . .
Lord, open my heart to your love . . .

After a long, deep silence to let themselves become truly open, they would say 'Lord, open our lips, and our mouth shall declare your praise.'

Aidan knew well the folk tales and legends of his homeland, among them the curse of the 'stray sod'. It was said that in a field there is a certain sod of grass which, if you stand on it, will trap you there forever. Those who by chance or accident step on such a sod will remain in the field and never escape. It was only a tale, but Aidan knew it described a reality. He knew of lives that had become closed, of people who had become trapped by habits and routine, people who had become possessed by possessions. He knew of grasping hands that were always closed tight, and hearts that were the same. He thanked God for Oswald and his generous life, and prayed that his hand might be open forever.

### EXERCISES

'Oswald was always wonderfully humble, kindly and generous to the poor and strangers.' Bede 3.6

1. Psalm 113.1–8. Repeat this psalm as a praise for the coming of Jesus, who came down for us and for our salvation, who came not to be served but to serve.

Praise the Lord.
O sing praises, you that are his servants:
   O praise the name of the Lord.
Let the name of the Lord be blessed:
   from this time forward and forever.
From the rising of the sun to its going down:
   let the name of the Lord be praised.
The Lord is exalted over all the nations:
   and his glory is above the heavens.
Who can be likened to the Lord our God:
   in heaven or upon the earth,
who has his dwelling so high:
   yet condescends to look on things beneath?
He raises the lowly from the dust:
   and lifts the poor from out of the dungheap:
he gives them a place among the princes:
   even among the princes of his people.

2. READ, RUMINATE, REFLECT, RESOLVE

READ
Read Luke 12.15–22.

RUMINATE
Chew over the parable. It looked as if all was going

well with the rich man. Surely God was favouring him. All that he did prospered. He had a good balance at the time of harvest. The crops were excellent – and every credit to him. He had far more than he could cope with, far more than he needed. What should he do with the rest? He would build bigger and better barns. The neighbours would see he was prospering. He would store all his other goods as well. The future was looking very secure indeed. How easy it is to measure our lives by what we collect. How often we are looked on as successful if we have a good deal of money or possessions. But we are not measured by things. Jesus told us that a person's true life is not made up of the things he owns, no matter how rich he may be. Often our true wealth can be seen in how much we give away, in how we are open to others.

REFLECT
See if this is a mirror of how you live. How do you measure your life? We all know that we cannot take our worldly goods with us, so we should not be over-attached to them. Giving another person your attention is a good way of opening yourself up to God.

RESOLVE
Resolve to be more generous in the way you give of yourself, your time and your attention. Seek to be more open to the other who comes to you.

3. Pray:

Lord,
You enrich us with your goodness
You enrich us with your love
You enrich us with your presence.

Teach us to share your goodness with others,
To share your love with those whom we meet,
To give ourselves in service, as you give yourself
  to us.
For it is in giving that we receive,
In dying to self that we are given eternal life.

# 6

## *A Desert in the Ocean*

The singing of seals late in the evenings and early in the mornings seemed to complement the prayers and singing in church. As the seals sat upon the banks and let the tide rise around them, so each of the brothers immersed himself in the presence of God. Aidan was forever reminding them that they could not talk about God if they did not talk to Him. Much of the schooling had to be directed to the Presence and not to theories about Him. They had to deal with the reality of God in His world, and not in fantasy. This could come in no other way than by immersing oneself in God. As the chattering terns soared and dived, so the devotions in the little church rose and fell. They were part of the life around them. The flow, standing, and ebb of the tide became a rhythm in their way of living. Aidan was concerned that there was proper input, rest and outpouring of each life. Some were in danger of thinking they could pour themselves out forever. They were outgoing, ready for action, wanting to get on. He had seen too many become drained in this way. We cannot give out forever unless we are also looking in. Too many lives, and too many statements, become trivialized by too much action. There is need to be renewed, refreshed and restored.

Like many Celtic monks before him, Aidan had sought his desert in the ocean. Most of the world was looking for an ocean in the desert, never satisfied, always searching for more and more. They were always in need. Here on the island, in a strange way, were all the riches of the world. Here was beauty, here was the power of the Presence. These were not things to search after but to accept, to become aware of, to enjoy. There had to be input for this to happen, times of quiet, times of prayer, times of meditation. This had not to be output, though it was often work; it had to become the incoming tide of the love of God. Students and brothers had to wait in expectant silence, like a man waiting to see a bird. This demanded concentration and alertness, but it also needed silence and stillness. The stillness of the church made the roar of the sea sound soothing for much of the time.

There were other students and brothers who liked to rest all day, calling it prayer or meditation. But Aidan knew that a man could only absorb so much if he did not also pour it out. He knew it could be poured out in prayer for others, but, he felt in his heart, it had also to be expressed in loving action for others. Real rest was the balance between the two, prayer and action, as the tide stood for an hour between ebb and flow. Watching a little boat at anchor, Aidan could see at a glance whether the tide was ebbing or flowing. He knew by the way it was turning, by the direction it was pointing. He would surprise visitors by saying suddenly, 'The tide has turned, we will soon be able to go.' He could see at a glance when a student, or one of the seniors, needed to be guided to a tide change in their lives. He could immediately see if a person was at home with, and content with, God.

The school grew gradually. First, each of the brothers took on an *anamchara* – a cell mate. The young man would learn from his elder, by rote, the Psalms, all 150 of them, and a Gospel. He would learn these also in church through their regular repetition. He would learn on a journey with his *anamchara* the same psalms, hymns and spiritual songs. He would also learn how to approach people on the road and in their farm steadings, to talk to them naturally about the living God. They would share their faith and their food. Slowly but surely the junior would be allowed to take part, even if it was just reciting a psalm to start with. As the junior grew in knowledge and in prayer he would do more until at last he would be trusted to do it all. Now the junior would become a senior and have a junior to teach. Because this process took a long time, more monks had to be brought in from Iona and Ireland to teach the ever-increasing numbers of students.

Some of the students were destined to be monks and priests. Their studies would take years. It was necessary that they had a deep love for God, and a firm grasp of the scriptures. Because books were rare, much of the scriptures would have to be learned by heart. There was something very impressive about these men as they recited verse by verse from the Gospels. They were not men of books but of a living faith, a faith that came from inside them. Aidan would remind them again and again, 'You cannot bring out what you have not let be poured in.' There was something very striking about great words being poured out of simple men – words that came out of their hearts and vibrated in their lives.

The life of the monks expressed the rhythm of life around them. They would balance their lives between prayer, study, manual labour and rest. Those who were not of the studious kind would spend more time in physical labour. Such men maintained the very fabric of the community and made it possible for others to learn and achieve. Without the labouring brothers the outreach of the community and its hospitality would be severely hindered. Without the miller and the farmer, without the baker and the shepherd, mission would soon be brought to a halt. Every task was not only part of worship but a share in outreach and mission.

The students learned to write on tablets of wax. They learned art and mathematics on the same tablets. They learned about the preparation of skins for writing on. They discovered how to lay out a skin into four pages and to rule it with a stylus. They had to learn to be precise in the way they cut their pens from reeds or from goose feathers. Often progress was slow, but a firm foundation was being laid.

As the students were learning Latin, and a little of the Celtic language, the brothers from Iona were learning the language of the English. In the early days there was still a great deal of difficulty in communication, not only on the island, but in the community around. The English had one language and the British another, a common language between scholars was Latin and it helped to bridge a gap more than once. Aidan and his twelve were having to learn the language of these British Celts as well as learning English.

Students were set a task of writing on their tablets. Once the work was looked at, guided and corrected, the tablet was wiped clear. Just as the tide came in on the way across to the island and wiped away all trace of footprints and hoof marks, so a hand went over the wax and wiped away all traces of the work. So often a student must have put in a hard morning or afternoon of work to complete a few sentences or a pattern, to have it wiped away by his teacher. If only he could save more! This would not happen until he was proficient at his words and letters and allowed to write on a skin. Occasionally students wrote their thoughts on wax as an exercise in expression. Later some students were bold enough to do this on spare space in the books they constructed. We can well imagine a student seeing his day's work wiped away to vanish for ever, and wondering at it.

Because I am a learner, I write in wax.
All my efforts will be wiped away,
A day's work erased by the evening.
Nothing lasts.
The tide turns,
The moon rises and wanes,
A day's work is gone before the moth hours,
A clean tablet for the morning,
To start all over again.
Yet not as the person I was yesterday.
I have gained something in the pressing of the
    wax,
It has made an impression on me.
It has gone from the tablet,
But it remains in my heart and mind,
It is there in a new dexterity of my hand.
One day I will make a more lasting mark.
God, may it not be wiped out, but last forever.

In their study of St John they would hear, 'Truly, anyone who gives heed to what I say and puts his trust in him who sent me has hold of eternal life, and does not come up for judgement, but has already passed from death to life.' In the candle-lighting of the night prayers this was acted out: 'Jesus Christ the light of the world has conquered darkness. Christ is a light no darkness can put out.' The light shone in the darkness around them. Yet all knew of the terror that walked by night, all knew the fear of sudden death. Time and time again they prayed that they might not be wiped out like a tablet of wax.

Into this place of quiet poured visitors: king and royal family, visiting clerics, courtiers, local leaders, seekers. The island was just off the main road, that is the sea road, so it was not far from the daily traffic. Countless people crossed the sands on foot or on horseback. This in itself worried the monks. Too often people did not understand the tide and were in danger of getting caught or even drowned. More than one had lost their life to the incoming tide. To the south of the usual crossing there were quicksands. So it was decided to place small cairns as markers, to allow people to come in a reasonably straight line but respecting the dangers. This is how we often have to go through life; we all need markers and guides. On leaving the island, the river near the mainland was always the danger point. The monks tried to make sure that leaving visitors knew how long it would take them and were aware of the danger. In this world we are all set amid dangers and we need to heed those who have learned the way. If we ignore the experience of the past, we run great risks with our lives.

As people came in their hundreds, the desert was in danger of becoming a city. Aidan was being sought out by more and more people. The busier he became, the more time he needed to spend with God. The more he poured out, the more he needed to get away from it all and be renewed and restored. The need became more serious as the numbers increased and the guesthouse filled, and more people learned to stay over the tide. There were times when it seemed there was no escaping people, no hiding place. They seemed to interrupt everything. Aidan accepted that such invasions were the very thing he was here for. But he needed his quiet. The north shore of the island provided a good escape, but even here he was sought out. So he started going to the little Hobthrush island that was also tidal. It was only a few hundred yards from the monastery on the south-west corner of the island, but it was cut off by the tide twice in twenty-four hours. Here he built a beehive cell in the tradition of the Celtic hermits. He would share this place with the heron and the eider duck, then in the autumn, with the godwits, oystercatchers and other waders. The seals would come close to see what was occupying this little island which Aidan prepared by prayer and fasting. In the latter part of the year thousands of geese would also come around this small island.

Then the visitors started to come also. The little island was not far enough away to remain Aidan's desert. People hailed him from the shore. Monks shouted to say an important guest had arrived and needed to see him urgently. Some even came out on horseback or by coracle. Aidan knew he had to find somewhere further off as his special desert. On mentioning this to Oswald, they both saw that the answer was simple, another island.

The islands off Bamburgh were plentiful in number. Some were only small jagged rocks that disappeared at high tide. Some were full of sea birds and seals. None were thought to be habitable. It would seem that the nearest of the islands was the largest and most likely to sustain a tough way of living, but Oswald had his doubts. It was said that the island was inhabited by demons, small dark beings who put fear into any who had ventured there. Other members of the court swore that there were evil creatures there. They said that strange creatures lured ships to be stranded and the sailors drowned.

Aidan saw this as a challenge, and at the same time a witness to the power of God. He would go there and be alone. Through prayer he would ward off the demons and banish them from his desert in the ocean. This, he announced, was not a simple battle. It could not be done in a moment, it would take about six weeks. In one of the Lenten times, the Lent of Jesus, the Lent of Moses or the Lent of Elijah,[1] Aidan would go and fight off all that would harm. Oswald was a soldier and used to battles but he feared for Aidan. He had heard too many stories of marsh hags and sea monsters. He knew that there were so many things that could destroy a man. He knew also that Aidan was determined to live out the words, 'Be strong in the Lord and in the power of his might.'

Aidan asked that he might have supplies. He would not need much, and he hoped that in time he would manage to grow all he needed there. It could only be his desert if he could remain without too much help. He needed a place where he could truly have no one to speak to but God, a place where he could be still and know that he was enfolded in love.

So began the 'Desert in the Ocean'. Again Aidan spent times wrestling with the powers of darkness. There were nights on his own when strange sounds were heard. At other times it seemed as if great rocks were being thrown about. Now and again he wondered if he heard voices. He had to battle with the fears within himself as well as clearing the land of evil. Words he remembered from the Old Testament were an encouragement: 'The Lord himself has promised to be a wall of fire around the city to protect it, and that he will live there in all his glory' (Zechariah 2.5). He prayed that God would be known to him in all His glory.

This island helped Aidan to keep a balanced life. Whenever time allowed, he escaped there to be alone with God. Each season he planned to have some time there. Only in this way could he give God the priority He is due. It was also a good witness to the importance of prayer. These were turbulent times. Aidan prayed often for peace and the spread of the gospel.

Once, when he was on this island, he saw a lot of activity going on at Bamburgh. An army was marching towards the city. He knew by their attitude that they were invaders. It did not take much to guess that it would be Penda with his Mercian army on the warpath. Aidan hoped that the people of the village had fled into the fortress, for Penda would show no mercy. Bamburgh was so well defended by its rocky approach that Aidan was almost sure Oswald was safe.

However, Penda was tearing the village to pieces. He ripped the thatch off the cottages, pulled out beams, rafters and the wattle walls and had them carried up to the palace gates. Here a great heap was made so that they could burn down the gate and wooden wall and so break into the palace. The wind was favourable to Penda. He ordered the fire to be lit. Soon the palisade would be ablaze. Smoke was blown into the palace and high into the air. Inside the palace, eyes were streaming with smoke, others were already suffering from inhaling so much. There were signs of excitement and joy from Penda and his warriors. Soon another king of Northumbria would be no more. Soon Penda would be inside Oswald's great fortress.

Aidan, two miles away, saw the smoke rising and guessed at the trouble. The tide was about to turn and the wind was veering from the south-west. Tears flowed from Aidan's eyes. How easily all his good work could come to an end. 'The Lord himself has promised to be a wall of fire around the city to protect it!' The words came with difficulty. Then in a loud voice Aidan simply cried in despair, 'Lord see what evil Penda does.' As he spoke, he felt a change in the air around him. The wind suddenly changed direction, it was now blowing from the north-east. With joy he watched the smoke being blown away from the palace and across the land.

Penda's troops were no longer joyful. Their eyes and lungs were filled with smoke. The great billows of smoke were now defending the castle and blowing at them. It was as if the very elements had turned against them. It was no use staying there. They would have to leave. But they would return another day.

Aidan continued in silent prayer and thanksgiving. If only people would learn the power of prayer! If only they would learn to 'be strong in the Lord'!

### EXERCISES

'Aidan was living on Farne Island, which lies nearly two miles from the city, and which was his retreat

when he wished to pray alone and undisturbed.'
Bede 3.16

1. Psalm 130. Recite this Psalm, thinking of Aidan on Farne. Then ask how much time you set aside for God.

> Out of the depths have I called to you, O Lord:
>> Lord, hear my voice:
> O let your ears consider well:
>> the voice of my supplication.
> If you, Lord, should note what we do wrong:
>> who then, O Lord, could stand?
> But there is forgiveness with you:
>> so that you shall be feared.
> I wait for the Lord; my soul waits for him:
>> and in his word is my hope.
> My soul looks for the Lord:
>> more than watchmen for the morning,
>> more, I say, than watchmen for the morning.
> O Israel, trust in the Lord, for with the Lord there is mercy:
>> and with him is ample redemption.
> He will redeem Israel:
>> from the multitude of his sins.

2. Read Mark 1.35.

Before all the major events in His life, Jesus is found at prayer. He seeks to do nothing new without relating to the Father. Notice how He had to get up early. He had to escape from the house and find a lonely place. For Jesus, action without prayer was unthinkable. How much time do you spend in prayer? Is communion with God truly a priority in your life? Promise to set aside a time – and a place – for God.

3. Pray:

> Blessed are you, Lord God of all creation.
> You give me life
> You give me love
> You give me yourself.
> Help me this day
> To give my life
> To give my love
> To give my whole self to you,
> Father, Son and Holy Spirit.

## 7

## *The Open Hand*

Aidan watched Oswald at prayer. The king set a good example to his subjects. Aidan had realized from the start that there would have been no progress in the kingdom of Northumbria if Oswald and his thanes had opposed him. Oswald's open hands on his knees were a sign of the welcome he gave Aidan. Not only had he given lands and goods, he had given protection. He had ordered his people to accept the comings and goings of these monks, and to make them welcome. Aidan knew the Christian faith could not easily progress in a country when the leaders were against it. For a kingdom to be won for Christ you have to win its government and its leaders. It was more than good fortune that many of Oswald's thanes had spent time with him in Iona and Ireland. Already members of the court were reasonably committed, though he could think of one or two exceptions. Some of these Angles did not want to lose their old ways and their old traditions. More than once he had been reminded that the name Oswald meant 'Woden's ruler', and that the king was said to be descended from the god Woden. Aidan tried to tell them that they were all sons and daughters of God; not only did the king come from God, we all come from God. Everyone is important, for all are children of God.

In this openness and interchange, one of the thanes told Aidan of an old tradition concerning Woden. It said of him:

> I hung on a wind-blown tree
> For nine nights and days,
> I was pierced with a spear
> and given to Woden,
> myself given to myself.

Aidan could hardly believe what he heard, it sounded so much like the crucifixion. He talked long of the Christ who died on the tree, of the three-day burial and the mighty resurrection. Aidan told how this Christ was a mighty warrior, how he also was pierced with a spear, how he triumphed over the evil one and conquered the great enemy, death.

At the mention of defeating death, the thanes wanted to hear more, and so did others who were in the hall at the time. One of the singers offered a song about the passing of life:

> All will pass away.
> Money will pass,
> Wealth will pass away.
> Friends will pass,
> Companions will pass away.
> Strength will pass,
> Power will pass away.
> Security will pass,
> Life will pass away.
> Everything will pass,
> All will pass away.

Aidan felt the sadness in this song; it was about a people with no future, no hope, for whom nothing lasted. He wanted to tell them that this is not the way of Christ. He asked the singer to pluck gently on the strings of his harp. Aidan then began to chant:

> I look for the time,
> The glorious time,
> When the Lord's cross
> Will deliver me.
> He will take me

95

From all that passes
To that which is eternal;
Beyond darkness
Beyond death
Beyond the fires of hell
To that which is eternal,
Where there is joy
Where there is peace
Where there is love
Where there is glory
Where the saints do dwell
In life everlasting.

As his song ended, Aidan was given a rousing cheer. They wanted to hear more about this mighty God and the power of the cross. They wanted to know more about the life which is eternal. Aidan thrilled at their desire for learning and their openness to the gospel. It was one of those good moments that would have repercussions for a long time. He was fortunate to find these men so ready to learn. Not having heard the gospel before, they were readily open to its message.

On another occasion, Aidan was told how Edwin had become a Christian at the birth of his daughter. The hours before the birth were full of business as usual. From the south came a messenger called Eumer, claiming to bear an urgent message for the king. He was let into the king's presence and proceeded to produce a document from his tunic. But it was not a document but a poisoned dagger. His true mission was to kill the king. He was a trained assassin and his movements were rapid. No one had time to draw a sword. Only Lilla, the king's counsellor and friend, who was standing nearby, had time to act. He threw himself between the assassin's blade and the king. The faithful thane died immediately. The king still received a minor wound as the dagger passed right through the body of Lilla, and from this it took him some time to recover. He promised that, if he recovered, he would accept the Christian God as his God. Yet another faithful attendant was killed before the killer was dispatched. 'We are not afraid to lay down our lives for our king,' the warriors boasted, 'This is the highest honour, to die for him we serve.'

Aidan was moved by the simple heroics of these men. He told them how he too served a King and was willing to die for Him. He told of how many disciples had laid down their lives for this King. Christ the King asks for our loyalty and obedience. Aidan told of how his group from Iona called themselves 'soldiers of Christ'. He told how they had pledged themselves to withdraw from ordinary life and live on camp, ever ready to go out on mission. The measure of his men's obedience was 'even unto death'. They would go at a moment's notice on long journeys across savage country. They braved wild animals and fierce people, all for the love of God. They would continue until the kingdoms of the world became the kingdom of Christ, the kingdom of God.

As he told this to the soldiers they could respect him, for they could see that he was a warrior. He had a body and mind honed sharp by discipline and exercise. He had a spirit that was not easily daunted, strengthened by prayer and meditation. He was a strong, lean-looking man, obviously a man of action. The tonsure, which shaved off his hair from ear to ear, so there was none at the front and it grew long at the back, gave him and his men the appearance of being special. They were obviously men set apart.

Aidan continued to tell how his King had laid down his own life for us. Just as Oswald's men expected their leader to die fighting, so the Christ had died for all peoples. If he had so chosen he could have escaped, but for love he gave his life for all. In dying, he won a kingdom for his followers. So Christians have a definite purpose for living, to serve Christ and to live to the glory of God in doing His will. They also have a definite reward. Soldiers on earth can only be rewarded if the king is the victor. Christ has won the victory, and the reward is that we are given the kingdom of heaven. Life is eternal, man is free, for Christ has won the victory.

Aidan was well aware that it was Oswald's open door and open hand that allowed him such easy entrance into the palace and the kingdom. So now he watched in sadness as the king spent longer than usual in his prayers, because he was off on a campaign. Once again Penda was being a threat. Earthly kingdoms and all things that we build on earth are so fragile, 'all will pass away'. At this thought Aidan made the sign of the cross and prayed that Oswald would return in victory. It saddened him that the summer months were often the most violent. Summer is a time when troops can move more easily and so there were more raids and more battles. Oswald had decided to drive Penda back from his southern borders and if possible to conquer him once and for all. There could be no peace in the kingdom if this old warrior was allowed to make raids and cause such dis-ease.

The next weeks were anxious ones; there was

no news of the troops. The last that was heard was that they had gone further west and were deep into Penda's kingdom. Then more news came. Oswald had been victorious and had forced Penda to retreat into Wales. Oswald was camping after his triumph and was soon to come north. Soon the king would be home. That was the last of the good news. At home they were hopeful but they knew that winning a battle was not winning the war.

Meanwhile, Penda had persuaded the Welsh that Oswald would threaten them next. He amassed a new and powerful army from the Welsh of the borders. Oswald, still resting after his victory, was almost caught unawares. Wisdom would have counselled him to flee and fight another day. But Oswald had defeated larger armies before, and he could do so again. It was not in the nature of the Anglo-Saxon kings to flee from the battlefield. Oswald had lived heroically and if necessary would die a hero. The opposing army called him 'Bright Blade'; he could not tarnish his name by fleeing the battle.

The battle was one of great fury, and many good men lost their lives. It soon became apparent that it was going against Oswald and his warriors. One after another of the men around Oswald were cut down. Soon there was only a small band protecting their king. They surrounded him and made a human shield to defend him. These were mighty warriors. But they were being felled one by one. Oswald knew he would soon die for the cause he had lived for, the kingdom of Northumbria and the kingdom of God. Shields clashed, swords vibrated loudly. The foes were closing in fast, Oswald knew he was about to be slain. Amidst the clanging of metal, he uttered his final prayer to God as a great sword struck his head. He prayed for his men in their last battle, 'God have mercy on their souls.' It was the 5th of August in the year 642. Oswald had reigned for nine years and helped to maintain a fragile peace. Now, at thirty-eight years old, he was sent to his Maker.

Penda, triumphant, stood gloating over the body of Oswald. This was another of those Christian kings defeated. He cut off Oswald's head and rode with it through his ranks victorious. He ordered Oswald's arms and hands to be also cut off. The head, arms and hands were impaled on spikes and displayed at the hill fort of Hen Dinas, as a symbol of the triumph of the ancient gods.

All this was reported to the royal court at Bamburgh and to Aidan by one of the few who escaped to tell the tale. The same day in the great hall there was much keening. A singer described the lonely heights where Oswald's body lay. The picture he painted was full of doom and without Christian hope.

> Tonight the mead hall is deserted,
> No giving of rings or sharing of treasures,
> No drinking of mead or feasting on food.
> The king is gone, not to return,
> Our noble one is hung on a tree.
> There in the night with owl cry,
> There the wolf will gnaw him,
> The grey moorland wanderer eat him.
> There the raven will raid him,
> The black-coated one take an eye from him.
> They tear at the lifeless one,
> They pick at our noble one.
> His hands cannot drive off these warriors.

His life is poured out and all hope is gone.
Pale on the spike he endures his fate.
Mists, the shrouds of death, surround him.
So sad for us, we have lost our dear one,
Gone far from us our noble one.
Our king is on the gallows tree.

All present were touched with heaviness and sadness. Aidan himself was seen to wipe away tears. Oswald, who had been wonderfully humble, the kind and generous king, had departed. The open hand had been torn from his body and was out in some mist-strewn hill country. Aidan's heart ached for Oswald, and for the future of the Christian mission.

Aidan offered up prayers for the king in Bamburgh, at the palace and in the little church. He offered up prayers on Lindisfarne and on Farne Island. He encouraged his people to hold fast: 'We may lose round after round, but we know that victory is ours. We may lose each campaign and feel greatly defeated, but remember, death itself is conquered; we are free, for Christ has won the victory. Nothing can separate us from the love of God in Christ Jesus. In Him we are more than conquerors. As we think of our loved ones departed, let us say, 'The souls of the righteous are in the hands of God.'

Aidan believed all that he said, he knew it was right to restore confidence and faith to the people around him, but he was afraid that hard times would now come. Penda was not known for his mercy. The minstrel's song kept coming to his mind: 'All will pass away'. Slowly and deliberately, he made the sign of the cross, the sign of salvation. With a raised voice he proclaimed the words from

St John's Gospel: 'God so loved the world, that he gave his only Son, so that everyone who believes in him may not die but have eternal life.'

**EXERCISES**

'It is said that Oswald often remained in prayer from the early hour of Lauds until dawn, and that through his practice of constant prayer and thanksgiving to God, he always sat with his hands palm upwards on his knees. It is also said, and has since become a proverb, that "His life closed in prayer"; for when he saw the enemy forces surrounding him and knew his end was near, he prayed for the souls of his soldiers, saying as he fell, "God have mercy on their souls."'
Bede 3.12

1. Psalm 103.1–5

Praise the Lord, O my soul:
    and all that is within me, praise his holy name.
Praise the Lord, O my soul:
    and forget not all his benefits,
who forgives all your sin:
    and heals all your infirmities,
who redeems your life from the Pit:
    and crowns you with mercy and compassion;
who satisfies your being with good things:
    so that your youth is renewed like an eagle's.

## 2. READ
Read Luke 9.23–4.

### RUMINATE
Jesus has just been talking of his own willingness to give Himself completely, to die for us. He asks that we are willing to pour out our lives for others. Picture Christ dying on the cross and know that it is out of love for you. See his arms opened wide. Know that the nail-torn hands are open for you. Know that the riven side is opened for you. His heart, His love reaches out to you. It is this Christ who says, 'Give and it shall be given unto you.' It is this Christ who calls us to follow his example.

### REFLECT
Think of all the people who have enriched your life by their goodness and sacrifice. Quietly give thanks for each one of them, those who brought you into this world and cared for you, those who taught you and inspired you, those who gave themselves that the world might be better for you.

Give thanks that 'God so loved the world that he gave ...' God's love, God's life, God's very being, is reflected in our giving.

What profit is there in amassing things and being spiritually bankrupt? To fill our lives with possessions and activities is no alternative to having a lively spirit.

### REACT
Give time, give attention, give yourself to others and to your God. Check each evening to see how you have done this. God gives to us that we may give to others.

3. Pray:

Lord,
You give me life
You give me love
You give me joy
You give me peace
You give me yourself.
In you I am enriched.
Help me to share,
To give of what I receive.
Help me to give my life
To give my love
To give myself
In the service of others
And to you, Giver of all.

## *The Common Touch*

'If you are to meet people you need to have your feet on the ground.' This was something Aidan was always instilling into his students. He was referring to the choice between riding a horse or walking. He would insist that riding on a horse puts you five feet above everyone you meet. 'Walk when ever you can; riding separates you from people. Even if a few of you are riding, it is harder to talk to each other on horseback than when walking. Walk and talk. Whenever you meet someone, talk to them, share with them what you have received. Share your food and your faith. If they are Christians, share your faith with them, and pray together. If they are not, bring them the riches of the gospel.' Walking is a good pace for reciting the Psalms and for sharing your faith!

We may imagine Aidan giving instructions to the brothers as they set out on a mission – instructions which we ourselves might well take to heart, with a little adaptation, in a later century.

'Keep your feet on the ground, and keep life simple. It is no use our giving up material possessions and land, only to take on board complex ideas and intricate acts of worship. Keep it all simple. Let the gospel – no, let the Lord – speak for Himself. Introduce people to Him and bring Him to them, but then they must be encouraged to take up a relationship with each other. That is the only road to a true faith. Faith is a relationship with the living Lord. Encourage people to speak to Him, for it is the only way they will really get to know Him. Let people see that they too can have a relationship with our Lord.

'Encourage simple prayers of few words. They must be able to pray whilst they milk their cows or tend their sheep. So the words need to be few and

106

direct. They need to be able to pray when out at sea or in the forest, so they need to carry their prayers around in their hearts. Give them short sentences that they can take away with them. A few words, often repeated and from the heart, are worth more than many long prayers. Encourage them to repeat them over and over until they resonate in their lives. Repetition directs the mind. It is good for fixing patterns and creating certain responses.

'Teach them to fill their lives with good, deep, meaningful affirmations about God and his world. Let the words be loud on their lips, the very vibrations give them strength. Teach "Maranatha – Come, Lord Jesus". Encourage them to say it morning and evening, not to bring Him down but to lift themselves up. Not to make anything happen, but to affirm the reality of what actually happens. Not to make God act, but to open up to His coming. "Maranatha – Come, Lord Jesus." Encourage them to accept the fact that He is there with them. He is in their huts and in their fields. Jesus has said, "You will die in your sins, if you do not believe that I am." We must help them to meet with the living Lord, with the great I AM. So again invite Him into their presence. "Maranatha – Come, Lord Jesus."

'Get them to move the words from their lips into their mind. Keep dropping the words in like water dripping into a pool, until it fills them to overflowing. Use images, visualize, picture. Tell them: "See that the Lord is with you. He is there at your side. He is with you on your journey. He shares your room. He is with you in darkness and in light. If you cannot visualize this, open yourself to Him. Call upon Him: 'Maranatha – Come, Lord Jesus'. Focus on His presence, do not be distracted. Use the words to focus the mind. 'Maranatha – Come

Lord Jesus.'" Remind them that they do not need to be in church or on their knees to pray, for if they are alive God is with them. The mind and the imagination can tell them lies, can tell them God is not with them. But we know this is not true. God is with us all. Teach their minds the truth. Affirm the truth, that God is with us and loves us. Call upon Him; "Maranatha – Come, Lord Jesus."

'Slowly the words will move from the lips into the mind. From the mind they will reach into the heart. Suddenly, in the very depth of our being, we will know that "the lord is at hand", and that "in him we live and move and have our being". Now we will have reached a new level. The Lord who was without is now within; we are one with Him and He with us. In this way we will fulfil the great prayer of Jesus in St John's Gospel: "I pray that they may all be one, Father! May they be in us, just as you are in me and I am in you ... I in them and you in me." From the lips to the mind, from the mind to the heart – but all the time we must remember that it is the reality of the Presence we are about, the God in us meeting the God in them. Let the words resonate wherever you go until the living Word resonates in their lives. Keep it simple, and let the Lord speak for Himself.' Here Aidan might recall some words from Cassian: 'No one is being kept away from purity of heart by not being able to read, nor is its rustic simplicity any obstacle to it, for it lies close at hand for all. If only they will by constant repetition of the phrase keep mind and heart attuned to God.'[1]

Simplicity of prayer and simplicity of life helped Aidan and his followers to reach out throughout the kingdom. Wherever any priest or monk visited, he was made welcome. Whilst on the road people would run up to the brothers and seek a blessing. Folk were eager to be signed with the saving symbol of the cross, praying that the mighty God would protect them. Aidan would always remind them that a blessing was not magic, it was a reality. A blessing is a sign of what God has done and is doing to us and for us. Wherever Aidan went and spoke, he received an attentive hearing, the way was open for the gospel. People gathered by streams to be baptized and to sing praises to God. They gathered in cottages and bothies to hear with joy the word of God and to pray. The sick were tended and prayed for, the oppressed were brought relief. Whatever the need, Aidan and his men sought to meet it. More and more people recognized that these men lived as they taught, their lives were their teaching. They continued to give away any riches they received and to minister to the poor. Throughout their travels they went on foot unless necessity compelled them to go on horseback. When a monk was leaving on horseback he would often hear Aidan say, 'Get your feet on the ground as soon as possible; it is not good for you to be above the people that you meet. Remember that you are here to serve them and not to lord it over them.'

There came a time when this teaching would be tested. Some time after the death of Oswald, Aidan was at the palace of King Oswin who succeeded him in Deira. Oswin was a truly noble king, handsome in appearance, tall in stature, pleasant in his speech and courteous in his manners. He was known for his generosity in giving to rich and poor alike. This was one of the positive characteristics of the Angle and Saxon kings – they were expected to be generous. A king would be judged by his willingness to give, though often it was from booty. Oswin won the affection of many by his kindness and his regal qualities of mind and body. From all over the province nobles came to serve him. He was also respected for his humility, which was a characteristic often missing in the royal court. Oswin gave Aidan a very fine horse. The king felt that it was not right that Aidan should walk such great distances. Not only was it tiring, it was costly in time. The Deiran capital was far from Aidan's Lindisfarne home. It was nearly 150 miles of diffi-cult walking. Aidan insisted that he wanted to visit places on the way and to meet as many people as he could. Oswin, however, felt it was beneath the dignity of a bishop to be walking like a peasant; a man must accept his elevated position if he is to wield any authority.

Aidan did not see it this way. Time and time again he had been enriched on his journeying by the people he had met. It was through these chance encounters that he had been able to spread the gospel among the common people. If you are walking for a few hours with a person, it is amaz-ing how much you can communicate. However, to please the king he agreed to take a horse. Yes, it would be quicker and he would arrive at his desti-nation earlier. There were indeed great advantages in being able to travel quickly, and Aidan was an experienced horseman. Oswin himself took Aidan to the stables and selected one of the finest horses. If it was for the bishop it had to be the best. The same reasoning went into the choice of the harness, reins, and saddle. These were not just of the best leather, they were decked with silver and precious stones. All this was fitting for a prince of the church. Oswin was very generous towards all that Lindisfarne was doing and achieving in his kingdom. He also insisted that a man in Aidan's position should be seen to be important.

Aidan was grateful, if not overawed by such a gift. He knew that one or two of the brothers would be delighted. At least one of the younger monks had been trying to get him to ride more often. The same monk wanted him to take on a more dignified role. Yet, the minute he left Oswin's palace Aidan was uncomfortable. He knew he should not be; the saddle was of the best and the most comfortable anyone could imagine. As he passed people at the palace gate some bowed in deference to him. He already felt that he was high above them. There was a little group of peasants going in the same direction, but he soon left them behind. Anyhow he could have hardly walked with them and led his horse. The way some of them eyed the horse and its trappings, Aidan knew he would need an army to protect it. Once into the forests, robbers would be very interested in all this wealth. He would be a target for jealousy and greed. Some wonderful craftsmanship had gone into making the saddle. The tooling of the leather and the stitching were of the best. The placing of ornament and the silverwork had been done by a true artist. The saddle alone would be worth a dozen slaves or even a small farm steading. Aidan wondered, 'How will I sleep tonight? I will need to stay awake to protect my property. Even in the daylight I will have to ride fast, in case the people I meet are robbers. I had better not stop more than I need.' A sadness crept into his heart; he was already allowing himself to become possessed, to

111

be separated from people by material things and by position. Being on horseback is a very exalted position.

But God had already solved his dilemma. Aidan had slowed down because of the heaviness of possessions weighing on his heart. As he turned a corner, away down the road in front of him was a beggar. The poor man had already noticed him and had taken up his pose of asking alms. Again all sorts of thoughts passed through Aidan's mind. What if this was a trick and the man wanted to rob him? 'Life is not just; here I am with all these riches and here is a man with nothing. How can I ignore him? To ride past him is to ride past the Christ. "As much as you did it to the least of these you did it to me."' What was happening to him? Already his heart was hardening. If he did not stop soon he would be past this poor man and an opportunity would be gone forever. Was he going to allow himself to become hardened to the needs of others? What if he never saw the man again? What if he met him on the judgement day and he said, 'I was hungry, but you did not feed me, I was thirsty and you did not give me drink, I was naked and you did not clothe me, I needed friendship and you ignored me'?

The beggar was startled as this important person suddenly reined his fine steed. The creature was just as startled and skidded to a halt. The man was amazed when the rider got off his horse. He expected this great man to speak in the language of the Angles but he spoke his own language, the language of the common people. Though the accent was a little strange, he had no difficulty in understanding. Aidan had little to give him, as usual he was travelling lightly. But his heart went out to this poor man. He took him by the hand and explained that he had little except the horse on which he rode. It was then that Aidan decided to give the man the saddle and all the fine trappings. Such a gift was beyond the man's dreams, they were worth a fortune. Aidan said he would give them to the man and he could sell them. At first a fear came into the beggar's eyes. This man must be mad, or was it a trick? No one had ever taken much notice of him before, and no one had ever offered him more than scraps. His eyes opened wide in fear and disbelief. Aidan embraced him, saying, 'Do not fear, brother, I seek to give what I can to you in the name of the Holy Three. I give to you as the Father gives you life. I give as the Son gives you love. I give as the Spirit gives you strength. As God gives you himself, I give you what I can.'

As Aidan turned and was about to remove the girth and saddle, at that moment he realized he would never manage the horse without its precious trappings. For a brief moment he stalled. He could not make the gift. The man could carry the saddle and bridle, but without them Aidan would never control this spirited animal. Then he saw the simplicity of it all. The man could have the horse as well. He turned once more and said, 'My brother, I have come to a new decision. I cannot give you part, I must give you all. Take the horse and all its trappings, for the love of God.' The beggar at first was not sure. He had never been rich enough to own a horse. He had never even ridden one. How would he manage? Aidan told him how to lead it, and where to take it to get a fair price. For a while they stood facing each other. Then Aidan reached out with his hand holding the reins and placed them in the beggar's. For a moment he embraced the beggar as he would a dear friend. Each looked the other in the face; both had tears in their eyes. The beggar went back in the direction of Oswin's city, walking in a more upright way than he had ever done in his life. Was it a madman he had met, or someone who had set him free for a new life? This man of God certainly would make him think more about the God who did care for all conditions of men.

Aidan started to walk, feeling a little light-headed and with heart aflame. His journey would now take longer, but he would meet more people. He would sleep easily at nights for he would not need to worry about the horse, he had nothing a robber would want. His only worry was what he would say to Oswin the next time he went to the palace.

As it happened it was not long before he returned to Oswin's court. He could see by the king's looks that he knew what Aidan had done with the horse. In fact the whole court had been shocked by the tale when it reached them. The king was hurt by the slight that had been put on his friendship and generosity, though he knew in his heart that if a man is truly given a gift, he is then free to do what he will with it. The time for them to dine was approaching when the king said, 'Aidan, what did you mean by giving away the horse that I gave you to be your very own? I have been told you gave it to a beggar. That horse was fit for a king, not for some vagabond. I could have found you an old nag if you wanted to give it away to the first person you met.' Aidan's quick reply stunned the hall to silence: 'What do you think, O King? Is the son of a mare worth more in your eyes than that son of God?' No one dared to speak; even the king was silent.

As the king went into the hall everyone followed, awaiting the reaction. Aidan took his seat.
Oswin, fresh from the chase, did not sit down but
warmed himself by the fire. It looked for a while as
if he would not come to the table. His loyal thanes
stood by him. He seemed lost in thought. Suddenly
he loosed his sword and gave it to a thane who
was near. The king knelt at Aidan's feet and asked
forgiveness. 'Never again will I mention this, or
pass judgement on how much of your money you
are giving to the "sons of God".' Aidan at once rose
from his seat. This was not a good position for the
king to be in with his thanes present; some of them
might not understand it and think the king weak.
Aidan suggested to the king that he sat down to eat
and no longer let the matter be a bother to him.
Oswin showed a beaming smile as he sat with
Aidan. Here was a man after his own heart; a pity
he could not stay in the palace and advise him.

Aidan, however, felt a chill in his heart. Here was
a noble king indeed, but he was not long for this
world. Aidan felt in his bones that something was
soon going to happen to the king. His whole being
filled with sadness and tears began to flow. The
priest who accompanied Aidan noticed his distress
and asked in the tongue of the Scots, 'Tell me,
Father, what is it that grieves you so?' Aidan quietly
replied, for the priest's ears only, 'I have never until
now met such a humble king. But I feel that he has
not long to live; for the people do not appreciate
such a ruler. I am sure that the king will die soon.'
Sadly for all, this prophecy would quickly come to
pass.

Aidan treated all alike as his brothers. He loved
all as children of God. He did not fear the mighty
or see himself above the lowliest. He instilled into

the brethren that we meet God in the other. We cannot love either God or our neighbour. We love both or neither. The worst kind of dualistic thought is to separate God from His creation. We meet Him in the other. A person's very 'otherness' speaks to us of the great Other who is God. We must let them come as they are, not as we would like them to be. In the strangeness of the stranger God comes and asks for wonder. We are not to change the otherness but to have reverence for it, not to manipulate but to accept, to love. Aidan was sure that when two people meet together it is also an encounter with God. No one is common, for everyone is a mystery, and if we give them proper attention, that mystery will unfold before us.

### EXERCISES

'When a poor man met the bishop and asked for alms, the bishop immediately dismounted and ordered the horse with all its royal trappings to be given to the beggar.' Bede 3.14

1. Psalm 145.1–9, 14–16. Think how gracious God is, and how much he has given to you. Know he asks you to share with others what you have richly received.

> I will exalt you, O God my king:
>> I will bless your name for ever and ever.
> Every day will I bless you:
>> and praise your name for ever and ever.

Great is the Lord, and wonderfully worthy to
be praised:
   his greatness is past searching out.
One generation shall praise your works to
another:
   and declare your mighty acts.
As for me, I will be talking of the glorious
splendour of your majesty:
   I will tell the story of your marvellous
   works.
Men shall recount the power of your terrible
deeds:
   and I will proclaim your greatness.
Their lips shall flow with the remembrance
of your abundant goodness:
   they shall shout for joy at your righteousness.
The Lord is gracious and compassionate:
   slow to anger and of great goodness.
The Lord is loving to every man:
   and his mercy is over all his works . . .
The Lord upholds all those who stumble:
   and raises up those that are bowed down.
The eyes of all look to you in hope:
   and you give them their food in due season;
you open wide your hand:
   and fill all things living with your bounteous
   gift.

2. Read Matthew 25.31–46.


PAUSE

Be still, and know that God is with you, and within you. He gives you life. He gives you love. He
gives you Himself. You need not do anything but
open yourself to Him. He wants you to dwell in
Him and He in you. Say quietly:

117

You, Lord are in my life,
Your presence fills it,
Your presence is peace

## PICTURE

Call to mind the poor and homeless of the world,
the street children and the refugees. Think of the
deprived in your area. Pick out some particular
cause or person. Try to see their need, feel their
poverty. You may be able to look at some pictures
from the magazine of a charity such as Christian Aid
or Shelter. Study the pictures and their surroundings.

## PONDER

Know that the Incarnation is a glorious mystery to
be enjoyed, that one of the great ways of seeing
God is to seek Him in the other person. You are
called to see Christ in others – and to be Christ to
others. Christ calls you to do His work and without
you some of the work of Christ will not be done.
In a mysterious way the Christ has made Himself
dependent on you. Know that he calls you in the
poor and the refugee. Know that, when you give
yourself to the other, you are sharing in the love of
God.

## PROMISE

Promise that you will seek and share with someone
worse off than yourself. Know that you are being
enriched by that person, and they are allowing you
to extend yourself in love.

## PRAY

You are the caller
You are the poor
You are the stranger at my door

You are the wanderer
The unfed
You are the homeless
With no bed
You are the man
Driven insane
You are the child
Crying in pain.

You are the other who comes to me
If I open to another, you are born in me.[2]

## *The Life that Vibrates*

Aidan was slowly tracing a pattern of Celtic knot-work, and thinking leisurely of what had been. So many lives and cultures had crossed and inter-related. There was no Scot, Pict or Celt, no Angle or Saxon; all were one in Christ. Christ had broken down the barriers that divided them. In Christ the nation was becoming more united. Even this art-work was deeply influenced by the exchange of cultures. The illumination of the Gospels coming out of the scriptorium was a blend of Celtic and Anglian or Saxon. They had greatly enriched each other. The movement from hostility to hospitality was enriching all. A thought flickered about the pagan Penda. Aidan saw that here was still a great danger. Penda could wipe out all the progress that had been made. Aidan sent up a little prayer for protection, 'Lord see what evil Penda does.' Aidan was in no doubt that the world was full of dangers; so many things could happen in these fragile kingdoms, he thought with longing, as his fingers rose out of tracing the Celtic knotwork.

Aidan remembered the day when four boys had been brought to Lindisfarne. They were four brothers from one family, all in steps and stairs, blond-headed and fair-skinned, like so many of the Angles. Yet he never quite thought of them as angelic, they were real lads, forever in the rough and tumble of life. Still, from the start they had been keen to learn and anxious to serve. They all had good English names: Cedd, Cynebil, Caelin and Chad. Their parents were rightly proud of them. Aidan recited their names in the order of their age. Cedd was the oldest and Chad the youngest. They were all young men of promise, though the oldest and the youngest had the most potential.

Aidan's thoughts turned especially to Chad. He

was the most scholarly. To get more teaching he had been sent to Ireland. There he had met quite a few of the famous teachers and learned much from them. The Irish monks were extremely generous in being willing to share all they had with any visiting scholars. They would lend them books as well as feed and board them for free. The Irish monks were still very necessary and important to the growth of the church and for its scholarship. These lads would go far; who knew, one day one or two of them might become bishops in the church. Aidan knew how important it was for mission to be local. If the church is to grow, its leaders must come from within its own community. Leadership must rise up from within, or the teaching will never truly take root. For any mission in depth it must be from the people of that area, reflecting the same ideas and values. Mission must always aim to grow locally. Such young lives full of promise and wanting to be shaped – what a wonderful gift. They would certainly have an effect on the people around them.

Chad seemed to imitate Aidan more than anyone. More than any of the others, he refused to ride a horse if he could walk. 'You must keep your feet on the ground, and not place yourself above people,' he would say, in a voice that was a good imitation of Aidan's. But he meant what he said, and it was hard to persuade him to ride. He, like Aidan, walked for mile upon mile, talking to all whom he met on the way.

Chad was always concerned for travellers, especially if a storm arose. The winds on Holy Island could be very violent. When the wind rushed from the Cheviots in the west, it was particularly strong. There were times when it was hard to stand upright, times when all the thatch was blown off the buildings. It was the north wind that piled up the sea and made it roar like an angry animal. On the nearby Farne Islands many ships came to grief. At the first sign of a strong wind, Chad would utter a prayer for travellers. If the wind increased, he would stop whatever he was doing and pray for the whole human race. He was deeply concerned that, if possible, none should come to harm. When a mighty storm arose and there was thunder, Chad would go to the church and pray in cross-vigil. With arms outstretched, he prayed that all would be delivered from destruction, from sin, from death and from judgement. He would seek to pray as long as the storm raged. Often he came out of such prayers exhausted. If anyone made a comment, he would say, 'Learn to pray until the tears come. Remember what the Saviour suffered for us, and for our salvation.'

Aidan traced a few of the ups and downs of the knotwork pattern. How like life it was, full of ups and downs, ins and outs, light and darkness. The pattern rose and fell, was open then went under and was hidden, again reflecting the openness and the hidden in our lives. 'That Christ may walk with us in the dark places and give us His light' – Aidan's heart ached with the love he had for these people. But he was aware of much darkness. Penda was still raiding Deira, and making inroads into Bernicia. Oswy was empire-building and that would soon cause trouble. There was still much tyranny and darkness to be conquered. It pained Aidan to think of how fragile it all was. He must commit himself more to trusting in God.

As his fingers rose on the pattern, he thought of all the good things that had happened. Boisil, a great scholar, and Eata, had started to attract many to the monastic house at Melrose. People were flocking there to learn and to worship. Its place on the river Tweed, and its distance inland, made it a great place for outreach and mission. Here was a very holy house indeed. More and more people were committing themselves to the religious life. More and more were seeing it as a heroic way to serve God. It was not an escape from the world but a deeper immersion into it. New communities were having to be built, new places of learning and new churches. All the way down the coast, at the mouths of rivers, little churches were springing up. A good few of these were within sight of the next, though still miles apart. It seemed that the kingdom was seeking to follow Christ. It was such a joy to visit these small worshipping communities. In many areas it seemed that the whole village was keen to commit itself to Christ and to peace.

Aidan's finger followed the pattern where it dipped under. He remembered that there was still much tyranny and violence, too many people still lived by the sword. Small communities were still at the mercy of raiders and robbers. The yellow plague was also ravaging parts of the kingdom, and that was no respecter of persons. In some areas whole villages were being wiped out. A few of the brothers had been lost this way. One or two of the brothers dedicated themselves to caring for those with the plague.

The pattern rose, and so did Aidan's spirit. There was Wilfrid, a clever lad indeed. He had come from Oswy's court and was a friend of the Queen Eanfled. He had come as a fourteen-year-old to look after Cudda, a Christian scholar and a close friend of Oswy. Cudda had suffered from paralysis and needed someone to care for him. He came to Lindisfarne bringing Wilfrid with him. Cudda taught Wilfrid Latin and the scriptures. The language that was still common to all was the Latin of the Bible. Cudda also filled Wilfrid with images of the church on the continent and at Rome. When Wilfrid heard of Chad going to Ireland for more teaching, he had declared he would rather go to Rome. Aidan moved quickly past a down on the pattern. He hoped Wilfrid would not cause any trouble. This young man seemed to be too interested in royal trappings and riches, in position and power. But Aidan did not want to create him in his own image.

Aidan's hand had wandered to the next dip in the pattern. The queen was insisting on keeping a chaplain from Kent and on keeping the continental reckoning of Easter. This could make things difficult at the palace. It would be absurd to keep two Easters, or for the king to have Easter and the queen to be still in Lent. It would cause trouble if one part of the court was celebrating Easter and the other Palm Sunday. It was only a matter of order but it ran deeply, and might cause pain. They would obviously have to have a Synod to resolve these matters. However, it was good that Eanfled was so committed to the faith.

Thinking of royal women, Aidan gave thanks for the growth in the vocation of women to the religious life. It did seem to be a good way for royal women to have a position of their own. Hild, at thirty-three, decided to become a nun. Here truly was a jewel for the church. She was deeply committed to the way taught from Lindisfarne. She had thought of going to France, to the sisters at Chelles, to be a nun. It was as well that she mentioned it to Aidan. He persuaded her that the church here needed people like her. If all the talent was going to the continent, how could the church here grow? Women's communities, and mixed communities, needed people who were used to leadership, and who had been Christians for a good while. Hild had all the qualities needed, and more. Hild listened to Aidan and decided to stay. She went to establish a new monastery on the north side of the Wear. Within a year she moved on to Hartlepool to replace the first nun in Northumbria, Heiu. Heiu was going further south to Tadcaster. All over Bernicia and Deira new communities were springing up. The land was being won for Christ. The Princess Hild would be a great gift to the church and the nation. She was a natural leader. Even now they were flocking to join her at Hartlepool.

On the next down of the pattern, Aidan thought of Ebba, sister of Oswald and Oswy. She was not happy in her marriage. She was a woman of great gifts, though not as strong as Hild. She also could give much to the church. As a natural leader, she should also be the founding mother of a house. Aidan prayed that the day would come, and that Ebba would be strong enough for the task. Ebba was a great woman of prayer and suited to a monastery rather than the royal court. But some things can only happen in their own good time if at all. Poor Ebba, it would free her from a lot of tension and misery.

Aidan looked at the pattern and thought of how vibrant it was with movement and colour. He glanced at the written words on the opposite page, '*Jesus est*'. Once again everything vibrated, this time with sound. He could hear in his memory the brothers in prayer on the road. So often they started with 'Jesus is'. Or with the more ominous,

'Unless you believe that I AM you will die in your sins.' It is so important that each of us makes this discovery, that 'Jesus is'. Aidan could hear it as clearly as if the brothers were with him. After he heard each statement Aidan again traced the pattern, rising with the words, and saying to the Christ after each statement 'Have mercy upon us':

'Jesus Christ'
'Jesus, Son of God'
'Jesus, Saviour'
'Jesus, Lord'
'Jesus, Redeemer'
'Jesus, Brother'
'Jesus, Bread of Life'
'Jesus, Light of the world'
'Jesus, Door of the sheep'
'Jesus, Good Shepherd'
'Jesus, the Resurrection and the Life'
'Jesus, the true Vine'
'Jesus, the Way'
'Jesus, the Truth'
'Jesus, the Life'
'Jesus, crucified'
'Jesus, dead'
'Jesus, buried'
'Jesus, risen'
'Jesus, ascended'
'Jesus, King of kings'
'Jesus, Lord of lords'
'Jesus, the same today'
'Jesus yesterday'
'Jesus for ever'
'Jesus before the foundation of the world'
'Jesus here and with us now'
'Jesus in eternity'

His own 'Lord, have mercy' helped him to travel past all the parts of the pattern that were going under. How like life, all these ups and downs, this weaving in and out. A peace was descending on Aidan, the sort of peace he felt each time he returned to Lindisfarne. There was a feeling of homecoming, of having been here before. Then he realized that he had followed the pattern around, and was back where he had started. Yet, it was not the same, he had changed in his travels. As he looked at the complex pattern, he knew that life was even more intricate than the Celtic design. He also saw that the pattern was endless, a symbol of eternity. For all its complexity, its ups and downs, this life is eternal. This is the gospel message, this is what helps us to rise. Aidan prayed that the island would be the place of his resurrection. He hoped that when he died he would be allowed to bless his brothers as Columba had blessed the community on Iona. He even wondered if one of the local horses might weep for him.

He was suddenly aware of the roaring of the sea and the piping of the oyster-catchers. He thanked God that he had been made so rich in people, that his life was so vibrant and colourful.

### EXERCISES

'Whenever any priest or monk paid a visit, he was joyfully welcomed by all as the servant of God. And if anyone met him on the road, they ran to him and bowed, eager to be signed by his hand, or receive a blessing from his lips. Whenever he spoke, he was given an attentive hearing, and on Sundays the people flocked to the churches and monasteries, not to obtain food but to hear the word of God taught.' Bede 3.26

1. Psalm 107.1–9 Think of all that God has given you and done for you as you say this psalm.

O give thanks to the Lord, for he is good:
    for his loving mercy is forever.
Let the Lord's redeemed say so:
    whom he has redeemed from the hand of
    the enemy,
and gathered from every land, from the east
and from the west:
    from the north and from the south.
Some went astray in the wilderness and in the
desert:
    and found no path to an inhabited city;
they were hungry and thirsty:
    and their heart fainted within them.
Then they cried to the Lord in their distress:
    and he took them out of their trouble.
He led them by the right path:
    till they came to an inhabited city.
Let them thank the Lord for his goodness:
    and for the wonders that he does for the
    children of men;
for he satisfies the thirsty:
    and fills the hungry with good things.

2. Read Mark 8.27–30.

PAUSE
Be still in the presence of God. Do not seek to do

130

anything, just be there and enjoy the fact that God is with you. Relax, know you have arrived, for God is with you and loves you. There is no need to achieve anything or do anything. Take heed of the words, 'Be still, and know that I am God.' If you are distracted, bring your mind quietly back and say, 'Christ is here.' Better still, just call him in love: 'Christ'.

PICTURE
See the disciples on the road or around a camp fire. They have been busy and a lot has been happening. This is a little time they share on their own. It is a time for Jesus to lead them forward and deepen their awareness. 'Who do people say I am?' Well, it is always easier to talk about others. They laugh when someone says, 'John the Baptist', they know he is not. Elijah, or one of the prophets, is cited in more hushed tones – well, it just might be. Then the sudden direct question: 'What about you? Who do you say I am?' Is there a silence? Does anyone else speak? Peter, impetuous as usual, blurts out, 'You are the Christ.' Feel the quiver in his voice and the shiver that goes down each spine. It is an earth-shaking reply. The Saviour, the Messiah, the Redeemer, the Hope of Israel – a thousand years of dreams and visions have become flesh and dwell among them. The mind cannot take it in, but the heart reacts, and knows. What more can be said? For the time being, too, many will not understand. Jesus asks them to tell no one.

PONDER
Think on the question, 'Who do you say I am?' You may like to look at the I AM statements in St John's Gospel to further this meditation (John 6.35; 8.12; 10.7; 10.11; 11.25; 14.6; 15.1) or just proceed as

below, adding statements of your own. Let the
answer be full of vibration.

> You are the Christ.
> You are the Chosen One.
> You are the Anointed One.
> You are the One that should come.
> You are my Saviour.
> You are my Lord.
> You are my God.

Utter each statement in love, and let others arise
from it.

PROMISE

Promise to let the name, the very presence, of
Christ, vibrate each day in your life. Promise that
you will call to him in love.

PRAY

> I believe, O Christ, that you are
> the Holy Son of the Father.
> I believe, O Christ, that you are
> the conqueror of darkness.
> I believe, O Christ, that you are
> the seeker of the lost.
> I believe, O Christ, that you are
> the risen and ascended Lord.
> I believe, O Christ, that you are
> here and with me now.

This prayer should have a rhythm – even a chord
played or a bell chimed after each 'I believe, O
Christ, that you are . . .' Then we should add our
statements. It is a good prayer for groups to pray in
a round. A new person takes up a set of two lines,
ideally adding their own statement in the second
line.

## *Seeing Beyond*

Aidan pondered over all the events that had quickly followed after Oswald's death. In Bernicia Oswy was immediately proclaimed king. There had never been any doubt that Oswy would rule the kingdom if Oswald was defeated or killed. It was fortunate that Oswy had been on a campaign in the north when Oswald went south. He naturally took over his brother's command. In the south Oswin took control of Deira, claiming the kingdom as rightful heir. So the great kingdom of Northumbria was fragmented once more. Aidan was relieved to know that both these rulers were favourable towards Lindisfarne and the Christian mission. Oswy, of course, had been on Iona with Oswald. He was a spirited leader who saw the benefits of having the Lindisfarne monks so near to him. He wanted Lindisfarne to continue and to flourish. He hoped for more schools and teaching for his leaders on their various estates. Aidan was free to go wherever he pleased and to continue his good works. All of this could only be for the benefit of the kingdom.

Oswy had a firm grasp of the faith from his schooling on Iona and then at Bamburgh. He sometimes amazed other leaders with his clear statements about God. His words were often the same, but they seemed to come from his heart:

God is boundless in his majesty, though
    invisible to the human eye.
God is Almighty, Creator of heaven and earth
    and of all the human race.
In justice he rules and will judge the world.
He abides in eternity, not in perishable metals
    and idols.
All who know and do the will of their Creator
    will receive eternal life.[1]

Aidan wondered how much of this had been learned from the singing of hymns and psalms in church. It made him think of the words popular on Iona:

> The Father exalted, the Ancient of days,
> Without beginning or ending, ever existing,
> Who is and shall be, to the ages of ages.
> All praise.
> With whom is the Christ, the only-begotten,
> And the great Spirit. Again let us praise.
> Co-eternal in glory, equal in Godhead,
> We preach not three but One God do we
> praise.
> We proclaim One and One only, eternally
> glorious,
> Yet have faith in the Three persons and
> gloriously praise.[2]

Aidan was greatly surprised when Oswy told him he was going to marry the Kentish princess Eanfled, the daughter of Edwin. Oswy already had a son, a love-child, born out of wedlock, Aldfrith, whose mother was an Irish princess called Fina, of the Ui Neill family. Aidan was friendly with her brother Finan whom he had worked with at Iona. It was already rumoured that one day Aldfrith could be king. Aidan was pleased at this thought, for Aldfrith was getting his schooling in the monasteries of Ireland. Oswy had later married Rhianmelt, 'Queen of Lightning', and so united the kingdom of Rheged with his kingdom. Of this marriage was born Alchfrith. Aidan had been told how the Queen of Lightning was the great-grand-daughter of Urien ap Rheged, the Christian king who had died trying to defend Lindisfarne from the pagans. It was a while since Rhianmelt had died and so Oswy was free to take Eanfled as his wife. Once more Oswy was aiming at a political alliance as much as a marriage. If he married Edwin's daughter, he would have a rightful claim to Deira.

Aidan smiled to himself as he thought of the priest Utta who had been sent to Kent to bring back Eanfled. Utta was a good horseman but not a sailor. He had gone to Kent on horseback, crossing the whole of Penda's territory. He could ride fast and lie low if necessary. He was chosen because he knew how to look after himself, but was important enough to bring the princess to Bernicia.

Utta had come to Aidan all of a tremble and distressed. What would he do if he met a storm at sea? Aidan lightly told him not to worry, Chad would pray for him and the princess.

This was not enough for Utta. 'I have suffered days of sickness and bitter heartache on the sea. The tang of the waves in my mouth and the movement of the boat distress me.'

Aidan suggested that he let someone else go for Eanfled. At this Utta was mortified; he could not turn aside this great honour for a bout of sea-sickness. 'I am aware of how small we are and how mighty the sea is. What I would like, father, is a blessing on my journey. Armed with your prayers, I will go more contentedly on my way.'

Aidan could see that Utta was genuinely afraid of the sea and its storms. 'I tell what we shall do, dear friend. I have here some oil; let us pray for God to bless it and give us peace.' Aidan blessed the oil and, dipping his thumb in the oil, signed Utta on the brow with the sign of the cross: 'The cross of Christ defend you from all evil.' Then he gave Utta the phial of oil, saying, 'Keep this close by you and let it be a sign of peace and calm. If a great storm arises, then pour the oil upon the troubled waters. Remember that Christ is in your ship, and call upon Him. Speak to Him who stilled the waves and calmed the wind. God be with you in your going out and in your returning. I can see that you will bring the princess and her retinue safely to Bamburgh. Do not be afraid, my brother; trust in God.'

Utta travelled with great speed to the palace of the Kentish king. A ship was prepared and all boarded safely. The princess had her own chaplain and some faithful attendants. Utta knew that the return journey would have to be by sea to keep out of reach of Penda. All went well. Utta clutched the phial of oil that hung from his belt, and it seemed to keep him calm. He regularly uttered prayers to the Mighty and Strong One. He prayed that he might know that Christ was in this boat. It seemed all was going to plan, and that his prayers were answered.

Suddenly it all changed. They were well up the coast when a great storm broke upon them. The sails had to be lowered. Planks were creaking and straining. Waves were crashing over the ship. Utta clung on to the phial. The day darkened and there was no sign of the storm ceasing. There was no harbour they could make for, they would have to ride out the storm on the open sea. The waves were horrendous. The vessel rose high then plunged down into the depths. All wondered how long they could survive. Even those who manned the vessel were expressing fear.

Utta decided this must be the moment to use the oil. He asked one of the crewmen to tie a rope to his waist and to tie the other end to the mast. Then, with great difficulty, he moved to the side of the ship. A great wave nearly swept him overboard. As the ship dipped, Utta poured the oil on the sea, and immediately the wind stopped and the waves eased; it all became calm. 'You have to believe me, father,' he reported. 'Ask any of those who were aboard. The moment I poured the oil on the troubled waters there was a calm. It was a miracle. No one on board knew what to say, except to thank God for their deliverance.'

Aidan smiled and said, 'We should all learn how to do this deed. There are many times in life when we are caught in storms and we let our faith waver. We need to trust in him who stilled the wind and calmed the waves. We need to learn to pour oil on troubled waters. Too often we perish in our actions because we are weak in our faith. We so easily forget that our God is always with us, and a very present help in trouble.'

Eanfled was a beautiful sixteen-year-old, fair-skinned with blonde hair. She was certainly a princess, having all the airs and graces of a ruler. She was used to being listened to and obeyed. With her came a good few of her ladies-in-waiting and attendants. All of them were Christians and committed to prayer. They showed a concern for the poor and a love of learning. Eanfled would be good for Oswy and a balance to his more warlike qualities. It was a pity, though, that they had brought their own priest with them. It would be dangerous to fragment the church which was still growing.

In the same year Oswy rode out on a special mission. He told no one where he and a small group of extra specially trained warriors were going, only that they would be away for a good while and no one was to worry. Aidan noticed that they went well armed but dressed not to be noticed. He hoped that they were not out to do some wicked deed. He prayed that their journey would be a safe one and free from warfare.

Oswy made his way as swiftly as possible across the kingdom of Penda to the very borders of Wales. He used the cover of night to creep up to the ramparts of Dun Dinas. They were not here for battle or booty, he was here to bring his brother home. It was not right that Oswald's remains were displayed by the pagan leader. It was not good for Northumbria that Penda could gloat over his victory. It was important that Oswald should be accorded the dignity he deserved. The Bernician warriors noted that the grass seemed to grow greener where the body of Oswald hung than anywhere else in the area. Each signed himself with the sign of the cross when they saw the gallows tree. Oswy wept silently as he placed the head and the arms in the leather carriers he had brought for this purpose. But there was no time for sorrow or rage, they had to be far away before morning light. They sped as fast as their steeds would carry them. Steaming horses and weary warriors did not rest until well into the day and deep into a forest. They still had a long journey before they would be home.

When they arrived at Bamburgh there was great rejoicing. Oswald was brought home in style. Silver-smiths were engaged to make silver shrines for the arms. These holy relics would be displayed in the Minster of St Peter in Bamburgh. Here pilgrims would soon come to be near the arm, and the hand that did not corrupt. Aidan had prayed that the hand would not perish and, though it looked pale, it remained quite wholesome. All remarked on this miracle, and said that Oswald was truly a saintly king. Northumbria now had a saint of its own, and one who fitted the nature of these Anglian peoples, a king who had laid down his life for his people, a man of courage and godly strength. The dynastic house that was said to have descended from Woden, had produced a saint of the one true God. Oswald would rally others to follow his example.

Aidan took the severed head to Lindisfarne. He could not help but feel all the Celtic tales of the good luck and protection such a head would bring. Here was the power and the energies of Oswald. Aidan saw how the skull seemed to shine. On one side was a hole of about three fingers' width. This had been the mortal blow. At least such a blow would have meant a swift death. Dear Oswald, how much he had done to forward the faith. Aidan decided that a shrine to Oswald at Bamburgh would be sufficient; that was the place of the rulers. The head he would bury, in case it attracted the wrong kind of worship. To have two shrines to Oswald so close to each other might only cause worldly rivalry. There was a little too much triumphal talk about Oswald for Aidan's comfort. Still, the head was given a place of special honour; it was buried inside the little wooden church where the brothers worshipped.

Deira was ruled by the last of the line of Aelle, Oswin. Oswin was generous to the church, giving it a holding on his estates and offering the monks freedom of travel. Oswin in his goodness was attracting scholars and artists to his kingdom. People were flocking to serve him in this land that was more hospitable than much of Bernicia. Churches and monasteries were spreading, and Aidan saw a good future, though the fact that Oswy was expanding his empire worried him. There was just a chance that one day he would rise against Oswin. Perhaps the fact that Oswin was Eanfled's cousin might stop this happening. However, the more Alchfrith grew, the more Oswy talked of a time when his son would rule the southern kingdom. He seemed set on the day when Northumbria would be united once more.

Oswin ruled for seven years. They were years of plenty, and he was loved by all, though some said he was too gentle and kind to rule for long. The qualities of gentleness and scholarship in leaders was not yet expected of the Angles, they had to be men of the sword. Oswy decided that the only way to be firm against Penda was to have a united kingdom, so he rode south against Oswin. The armies came together at Wilfar's Dun, ten miles north-west of Catterick. It was obvious that Oswy had a far stronger and more experienced army. The battle would go to the Bernicians. Oswin decided that it would be wrong to wage a full-scale battle and slaughter, so he disbanded his troops and sent them to their homes. He hoped that would prevent any bloodshed. But he knew that Oswy would be after his life – he had come from Bernicia with this sole purpose. Oswin decided to go into hiding with Tondhere, a close companion and nobleman. They went to the estate of a friend called Hunwald and hid in his house. They believed Hunwald to be a trusty friend, but Hunwald betrayed them to Oswy. From Oswy's camp the reeve Aethelwin was sent to assassinate both Tondhere and Oswin. Before the day closed, Oswin and Tondhere were dead. The day was the 20th August 651, and the place was Gilling. This action only alienated the peoples north and south of the Tyne.

News of this deed caused great grief at

Bamburgh. The feuding of relatives for power could destroy all that had been building up. War between parts of a kingdom could only bring down the kingdom. Eanfled was horrified by her husband's actions, and swore to Aidan that reparation would be made.

Aidan found the whole event hard to bear. Oswin had been such a fine, upright leader. His kingdom had been attracting all sorts of good and talented people. Deira was becoming a good place to live in. Now what would happen? Aidan's heart ached at the thought of all his good work coming to nought. He had spent sixteen years in Northumbria and there was still much violence and bloodshed. Kingdom was still fighting against kingdom. Christian was killing Christian. The powers of darkness were not far away, and were seeking to prevail. One had to be on guard all the time against the Evil One.

Aidan signed himself with the sign of the cross as a great wave of pain swept through his body. He felt as if his heart would burst for love of these tough Northumbrians. How much had happened, how much they had achieved! Throughout the kingdom there were now centres of learning and places of peace. Churches and monasteries were growing at an amazing rate. Only recently, there had come the news that even Penda would allow Christians into his kingdom. Penda too was looking for the stability and peace that such men and women could bring. The whole land seemed to be turning to Christ. No doubt that was why the powers of evil were seeking to triumph. Yet Aidan did not doubt that the kingdoms of this land were being claimed as kingdoms for Christ. A whole era of learning and artistic advancement was beginning. Church planting up and down the kingdoms was increasing month by month. A golden age was surely not far away. Aidan could see it happening. God was blessing His people and He was using Lindisfarne and its brothers to do it. Aidan's heart leaped for joy, his heart flamed with love. But how would he now face Oswy? Poor Oswin, Aidan had seen that he was not long for this world.

He made his way to the church of St Peter at Bamburgh, to give thanks for the lives of Oswald and Oswin, and to pray for Oswy. He would go to the place where Oswald's hand was enshrined. He would give thanks for all who had made his work possible. He would remember the holy Columba and the saints of Iona, he would recall those who had taught him the faith. He would give thanks for the brothers who worked with him and supported him throughout Northumbria. As he thought along these lines his heart filled with mingled joy and sorrow. So much done, so much still to achieve! He thought again of Oswin and the day that the humble king had knelt before him.

His heart pained him, and a darkness descended. The light had begun to fade, the long twilight of a late summer evening, but this was another darkness. He struggled towards the church. Each step felt as if his legs were made of stone. On the rise he could see Lindisfarne stretched out in the calm sea and the sun setting red to its left. There was a roaring in his head like the roaring of a mighty sea. He struggled to pray for his brothers on Lindisfarne. Truly that island had been the place of resurrection, the place where he had met and walked with the risen Lord.

The darkness clouded his sight, a pain stabbed deep inside. He was at the church but he could not walk to enter it. His legs refused to do what he wanted. His whole body shuddered with pain. He fell against the west wall. How long he lay he did not know; it did not seem long at all. Pain was blanking out all thought, it was coming like great sea waves. As a child he had been taught that the ninth wave is the big one, but he did not know how many times the pain swept over him. He was aware of helping hands, but they did not try to lift him. He was returning to the earth from whence he came. They built a little canopy over him, very like the covering he had had on some of his missions, to keep out the cooling night air. In gasps Aidan prayed aloud, first a prayer he had learned on Iona:

> My dearest Lord,
> You are a bright flame before me,
> A guiding star above me,
> A smooth path beneath me,
> A kindly shepherd behind me,
> today and evermore.[3]

Soon even words became difficult. He could only repeat, 'Jesus ... Jesus ... Jesus ...' A helpful young monk tried to get him to be silent. This was something Aidan could do with ease, but now he whispered, 'I have loudly proclaimed Christ with my whole life. If I cannot now shout His name, I will whisper it.'

Aidan felt God was calling him to go on yet one more mission. He was told that helpers were being sent. Assistance was coming from the castle, from up on high. But it would arrive too late, Aidan was moving away on another journey, with an escort of shining helpers. He was joining a new company, for angels had come for him. Suddenly all was light and brightness, his heart was aflame. He had left the kingdom of Northumbria for an everlasting kingdom. On the evening of the 31st August 651, Aidan entered that life which is eternal.

Even now, as the night descended, his torch for Christ was being handed on. Away to the north a young man, who was born about the time when Aidan came to Northumbria, was watching sheep by night. He had already been taught the faith by his foster-mother, a nun named Kenswith. He was looking to the south-east, as the sky grew dark and stars were appearing. It was then that he saw a vision of angels descending and ascending; on their upward journey they were taking a soul of great brightness into the kingdom of heaven. It was the next day that he learned that Aidan had died. Cuthbert knew he was called to continue the work that Aidan had begun; his heart was aflame with love for God.

### EXERCISES

'He cultivated peace and love, purity and humility; he was above anger and greed, and despised pride and conceit; he set himself to keep and teach the laws of God, and was diligent in study and in prayer ... I greatly admire all these things about Aidan.' Bede 3.17

1. Psalm 121. Seek to have a vision of a life that cannot be conquered, through Him who loves us. Recite this psalm as an act of faith.

I lift up my eyes to the hills:
　　but where shall I find help?

My help comes from the Lord:
    who has made heaven and earth.
He will not suffer your foot to stumble:
    and he who watches over you will not
    sleep.
Be sure he who has charge of Israel:
    will neither slumber nor sleep.
The Lord himself is your keeper:
    the Lord is your defence upon your right
    hand;
the sun shall not strike you by day:
    nor shall the moon by night.
The Lord will defend you from all evil:
    it is he who will guard your life.
The Lord will defend your going out and your
coming in:
    from this time forward for evermore.

2. Read Luke 19.35–43.

PAUSE
Close your eyes to distractions, close your ears to attractions, close your heart to temptations. Be still, and know that God is with you. Stay with your eyes closed. Know that the world has not disappeared. Know that God, though unseen, is ever near.

PICTURE
Visualize the scene. Jesus has descended to the lowest town in the world. They are just outside Jericho. By the side of the road there is a man in tatters and obviously blind. His other senses are not impaired, in fact they are heightened. Hear him ask, 'What's going on, what is happening?' The reply is deep: 'Jesus of Nazareth is passing by.' This is something he cannot miss, his whole future depends on it. The blind man clearly sees his

opportunity. He shouts, 'Jesus! Son of David! Take pity on me!' The crowd try to put him off, to quieten him. But the blind man recognizes his chance and shouts all the more, 'Son of David! Take pity on me!' Jesus hears and stops. He orders the blind man to be brought to him. What hopes and expectations must be rising for this blind man! Jesus does not force anything upon him but asks, 'What do you want me to do for you?'

'Sir, I want to see again.'

'Then see! Your faith has made you well.'

PONDER

How often our vision is impaired. We fail to see beyond our nose or beyond what immediately needs to be done. Do we realize how blind we are? So often Jesus of Nazareth has passed by and we have not noticed. We have allowed the crowd to silence us, we have allowed popular opinions to sway us. We need to extend our vision, to extend our way of living. God is not a God of diminishment but of extension. If we ask, and believe, our vision will be extended.

PROMISE

Promise that each day we will seek to expand our vision. We will look beyond the obvious and the immediate and seek to see our God at work. Seek each day to see God at work in His world.

PRAY

Lord God, who called Aidan to burn like a flame
   in the Dark Ages,
set our hearts on fire with your love,
open our eyes to your glory,
open our lives to your brightness,

147

and help us to show forth your light today;
through Christ our Lord, who is the Light of the
    world,
and reigns with you and the Holy Spirit, for
    evermore.

# Notes and Acknowledgements

The Psalms, and the extract from the service of Baptism (p. 12) are from *The Alternative Service Book 1980* of the Church of England, copyright © 1980 The Central Board of Finance of the Church of England, and are used by permission.

The quotations from Bede are taken from Leo Sherley-Price's translation of *A History of the English Church and People* (Penguin Classics 1955).

The quotations from the Rule of St Columba are taken from Lucy Menzies, *Saint Columba of Iona* (Dent 1920). The Rule is in the Burgundian Library at Brussels and was translated by Dr Reeves.

Prayers and poems which are not specifically attributed otherwise are the author's own compositions.

## CHAPTER 1   LIFE IS A BATTLE

1   C. S. Lewis, Introduction to *The Screwtape Letters* (Fount 1982).
2   *The Alternative Service Book 1980*, The Baptism of Children, p. 245.

## CHAPTER 2   THE OPEN DOOR

1   William Shakespeare, *Julius Caesar*, IV. iii.
2   From Kuno Meyer, trs., *Selections from Ancient Irish Poetry* (Constable 1928).
3   Copyright © 1989 The Iona Community.
4   From Robert Van De Weyer, *The Letters of Pelagius* (Arthur James 1995), p. 71. Pelagius was born in Britain during the mid-fourth century. He believed that church leaders should follow the example of Christ in humility and poverty. He was in Rome in 385 and much admired for his holiness and clarity of teaching.

He constantly emphasized the freedom of the individual. He did not believe that we cannot free ourselves from sin. Due to Augustine, Pelagius was declared a heretic and died in Egypt in 420. The teaching of Pelagius gives us an insight into the church in Britain in the fourth century.

5  Pierre Teilhard de Chardin, *Le Milieu Divin* (Fontana 1964), p. 64.

6  Columba converted Brude the arch king of the Picts whose fortress was at Inverness, and so won many of the Picts for Christ. On the journey to Inverness he met with the Loch Ness monster.

## CHAPTER 3  HEART AFLAME

1  G. M. S. Walker, *Sancti Columbani Opera* (Dublin Institute for Advanced Studies 1970), p. 97.

## CHAPTER 4  PREPARING THE GROUND

1  Although a quotation concerning Cedd, Bede says Cedd 'explained that it was the custom of those who had trained him in the rule of regular discipline to dedicate the site of any monastery to God with prayer and fasting' (3.23). In other words he was following the traditions he had learned from Lindisfarne.

## CHAPTER 6  A DESERT IN THE OCEAN

1  The Celtic Christians kept three special times of prayer and fasting. These were the 'Lent of Elijah' which was in winter and before Christmas, the 'Lent of Jesus' which was in spring and before Easter, and the 'Lent of Moses' which was in the summer and after Pentecost.

## CHAPTER 8  THE COMMON TOUCH

1  Cassian, *Conference* 10.14. Cassian was born in Romania *c.*360. He became a monk at Bethlehem, then

entered the desert in Egypt. In 415 he was ordained priest at Marseilles where he founded two monasteries, one for men and one for women. Through his writings, the *Institutes* and the *Conferences*, he brought the learning of the Desert Fathers to Gaul. His works were standard guides to the monastic life throughout the Middle Ages.

2  David Adam, *The Edge of Glory* (Triangle 1985), p. 34.


## CHAPTER 9  THE LIFE THAT VIBRATES

1  The quotation is about Colman and his predecessors, but it is a general comment about the effect of the Celtic mission and can therefore be applied to Aidan.


## CHAPTER 10  SEEING BEYOND

1  The author's own translation of Bede 3.22, words that are attributed to Oswy.

2  The first verse of the '*Altus Prosator*', a hymn attributed to St Columba of Iona. As well as being rhymed, the '*Altus*' has the first letter of every verse in alphabetical succession.

3  A prayer attributed to St Columba and found in many collections of Celtic prayer.

# Background Reading

Bradley, S. A. J. (ed.), *Anglo-Saxon Poetry* (Everyman 1995).

Colgrave, Bertram (ed.), *Two Lives of Saint Cuthbert* (Cambridge University Press 1985).

Colgrave, Bertram and Mynors, R. A. B. (eds.), *Bede's Ecclesiastical History of the English People* (Oxford University Press 1970).

Ellis, Peter Berresford, *Celt and Saxon* (Constable 1994).

Ellis, Peter Berresford, *Celtic Inheritance* (Constable 1992).

Finlay, Ian, *Columba* (Gollancz 1979).

Fryer, Alfred C., *Aidan, Apostle of England* (S. W. Partridge 1902).

Magnusson, Magnus, *Lindisfarne* (Oriel Press 1984).

Marsden, John, *The Illustrated Bede* (Guild Publishing 1989).

Marsden, John, *The Illustrated Columcille* (Macmillan 1991).

Marsden, John, *Northanhymbre Saga* (Kyle Cathie 1992).

Menzies, Lucy, *Saint Columba of Iona* (Dent 1920).

Pennar, Meirion (ed.), *Taliesin Poems* (Felinfach 1988).

Sharpe, Richard (trs.), *St Adamnan's Life of Saint Columba* (Penguin 1995).

Stanncliffe, Clare and Cambridge, Eric, *Oswald, Northumbrian King to European Saint* (Paul Watkins 1995).

Tranter, Nigel, *Columba* (Hodder & Stoughton 1987).